STATIONS OF THE

HOLOCAUST

JEAN LAMB

Dedicated to all the victims of the Holocaust and to those who resisted Nazi Terror.

Published by Jean Lamb
Copyright © 2015 Jean Lamb

Printed by W&G Baird,
Greystone Press,
Caulside Drive,
Antrim,
BT41 2RS
www.wgbaird.com

Printed in Great Britain

A catalogue record for this book is available from the British Library.

ISBN 978 0 9931742 0 9

Designed and set by Will McGrath
www.willmcgrath.co.uk

Contents

04   Coventry: The Journey Begins by John Witcombe

05   Exhibiting Stations of the Holocaust by David Moore

06   Forward by Jean Lamb

07   Preamble by Sister Mary Michael CHC

08   I   Jesus is condemned to death: the Jews are condemned to death

12   II   Jesus takes up his cross: the Jews are made to cart off their dead

16   III   Jesus falls for the first time: a boy is shot

20   IV   Jesus meets his mother for the last time: the Jewish mothers are separated from their children

24   V   Simon of Cyrene helps Jesus with the cross: a mother helps her dying child before the pits

28   VI   Veronica wipes the face of Jesus: Jesus sees the faces of the suffering children

32   VII   Jesus falls for the second time: the Jews are rounded up in the ghetto

36   VIII The weeping women of Jerusalem: woman fleeing with her children: children punished in the death camps

40   IX   Jesus falls for the third time: Jewish victims of experimentation in vats of freezing water

44   X   Jesus is disrobed: the destruction of all flesh

48   XI   The crucifixion of Jesus: the children are thrown into open fires

52   XII   Jesus dies for the whole world: the Jews bless one another before the ovens of Auschwitz

56   XIII The deposition of Jesus from the cross: the Jews are lined up to be shot and to fall into pits

60   XIV   Jesus is buried in the tomb: the archangel Michael calls the dead to rise from their graves

64   The Stations of the Cross and the Holocaust by Peter Doll

70   Stations of the Holocaust: A Jewish Reflection by Jonathan Wittenberg

74   References

76   Biographies

77   Acknowledgments

79   Artwork information

Coventry: The Journey Begins

I am delighted to be welcoming Jean Lamb to Coventry Cathedral for the opening of her Stations of the Holocaust exhibition. I have known Jean for many years and been a keen collector of her cast collections, which are evocative of the often troubling relationship between God and his people.

Her work is superficially naïve, but carries within it an extraordinary depth of prayerful preparation, reminiscent of iconography in the Orthodox tradition. I have followed the development of the Stations series, which have emerged from a wrestling with her own history and background, over a considerable period of time, and when Jean first suggested bringing them to Coventry for their official opening I was delighted. They mesh perfectly with the challenging history, art and architecture of the Cathedral, mirroring our refusal to deny the reality of human enmity and destruction, but at the same time acknowledging with wonder Christ's loving and suffering presence in the midst of that destruction, bringing hope for salvation.

The Coventry Cross of Nails is our particular icon of this faith, and has become a uniting symbol for a worldwide community of people committed to healing the wounds of history, learning to live with difference, to celebrate diversity and to build a culture of peace. I am very pleased that Rabbi Jonathan Wittenberg is providing a Jewish perspective for this catalogue: his sharing in this project shows the way that we can form bridges, especially through the medium of art, to enable us to journey forward together in these commitments.

We hope that your visit to the exhibition, or reading of this catalogue, inspires you in your own walk of peace, and that you will find in it resources for honesty, healing and hope – both as you reflect on the terrible history which the Stations represent, and on other contemporary wounds in our world's history, but also as you discover for yourself the love and strength that can enable hope to flourish, even in the midst of adversity.

John Witcombe
Dean of Coventry Cathedral

Exhibiting Stations of the Holocaust

I invited Jean Lamb to exhibit The Stations of the Holocaust at the 2004 Annual Methodist Conference with the Colloquy exhibition, held at Loughborough University. She showed the first five of her now completed fourteen Stations of the Holocaust and they were an integral visual part of the artistic gathering.

Two years later her ongoing project became a cornerstone of the Resisting Tyranny touring exhibition, which celebrated the 60th anniversary of the birth of Dietrich Bonhoeffer, travelling from its inaugural exhibition at Westminster Central Hall in January 2006, to Birmingham, Winchester, Milton Keynes, Bletchley Park and finally to Bradford Museum and Art Gallery.

During the London Olympics in 2012 Jean contributed to the Reaching Beyond exhibition held at Mile End Methodist Church with two of her new travelling versions of these Stations, cast in jesmonite plaster. Recently completed, they look and indeed are as captivating as the originals.

Jean's ability to weave together visual history separated by 2000 years and create an accessibility which challenges, invites, and questions with fascination and unease, is a measure of her skill as an artist, storyteller and commentator.

Within the British Methodist Church, visual storytelling is still making its way through the dominant speaking/singing culture. However, the Methodist Art Collection of twentieth and twenty first century religious painting is enabling churches to move beyond the spoken and embroidered word, to that of wonder within a visual mystery. Jean Lamb's work can hold its head high among such company, for it politicises a horror often domesticated and privatised by a spirituality unfamiliar with form.

The events surrounding the journey of Jesus with the cross are expressed and interwoven with the ethnic cleansing of the Nazi Holocaust. Soldiers, guns and army lorries share centre stage with mothers and children being separated and all this is placed alongside the mocking, whipping and falling of Jesus.

This work has an immediacy and a curiosity which never fails to draw me in: the colour, simplicity, honesty and horror of her project is compelling. It is not difficult to speak of the energy of Jean Lamb's narrative ability, but it is less easy to communicate in words the way in which she combines tenderness and brutality, innocence and betrayal, despair and hope. At first sight this project may appear to be at odds with the direct and unaffected way Jean speaks of her faith as a Christian minister.

Sadly, what she portrays is universally re-enacted by individuals, groups and nations.

Jean speaks elsewhere of her Anglo German heritage which adds yet another layer to the mystique of this remarkable work.

Reverend David Moore

Forward

The Stations of the Holocaust were carved between 1999 and 2012 in elm wood from one large log. The subject, though given to me in a moment of inspiration, had been weighing on me for many years. As an artist, I was a frequent visitor of the art galleries and churches in Germany and as a minister I had often led people through the Passion of Christ depicted in traditional Stations of the Cross. I became Artist in Residence between 1992 and 1995 at St Mary's Church in the Lace Market, Nottingham. It was there that I exhibited the work of Mietje Bontjes van Beek in 1995, whose sister Cato had been guillotined for Widerstand, resistance, to the Nazis in 1942. Later in 1995, I exhibited the work of the Jewish psychiatrist and sculptor Ismond Rosen in St Mary's Church. His figure work made visual reference to the Holocaust. Mietje's exhibition Versöhnung, Reconciliation, then travelled to Coventry Cathedral and Ismond's toured to the Kreuzkirche in Berlin.

During the Lents of 2000 to 2013, the last Station that had been carved was placed in the entrance foyer of the Convent of the Community of the Holy Cross for meditation and prayer during the period in which I was carving the next Station. Sister Mary Michael was especially drawn to the works and has contributed her Meditations besides each Station.

As the body of carvings grew, the Reverend David Moore from the Methodist Church, asked if he could use the Stations to exhibit around the country for the centenary of Dietrich Bonhoeffer, a German theologian who resisted the Nazis. Friends also asked if the Stations could be exhibited in their local Cathedral. With a wider audience in mind I began casting the Stations in 2014, in preparation for their first public showing in Coventry Cathedral, Lent 2015.

To assist with the theological context I asked Dr Peter Doll of Norwich Cathedral to write an essay detailing how the Stations are placed within a liturgical and theological framework. Rabbi Jonathan Wittenberg provides a Jewish perspective on viewing the atrocities of the Holocaust next to the cross.

This project would not have been possible without the loving support of my parents David and Annemarie Lamb, whose personal stories about the Second World War I listened to as a child. Mother was born in Pomerania, Germany, in 1926. Her family moved to Berlin in 1935, surviving Allied bombings and Russian occupation. My mother then came to England in 1948. My father was brought up in Clapham, London. His family were bombed out in 1941 and survived the many Doodle Bug flying bombs of 1944. My parents met at the Coronation Ball at St James' Hospital Balham in 1953, where my mother was training to be a midwife. They were married in Holy Trinity Church Clapham in May 1956.

As a Christian, I know that God's gift to us of Jesus could only have been brought about through the Jewish peoples. We learn from the Old Testament about God's character and purpose and we hear Jesus quote many texts, especially from Deuteronomy and Isaiah. Jesus has invited us all to share in the gift of a relationship with God, first given to Abraham. Through our common identity and experience of God's love, I hope that these images of the last hours of Jesus' life, set alongside images of the last hours of many Jewish people in the Holocaust, will speak not only of both terrors, but of the theology and hope we share.

Jean Lamb

Preamble

The human tongue stutters and stammers in the face of the enigma of life, its origin and end, meaning and purpose. The mind is stunned and the heart breaks: searching for an explanation, a response from 'Someone' who knows, 'Someone' to rectify. "O God, why?" each generation cries out, as it is successively overwhelmed by the weight of the suffering it is in turn called to bear, even amidst the seemingly fleeting joys and transient beauty of a world so full of promise and yet so agonisingly unfulfilled.

The Judeo Christian tradition is set firmly at the centre of this mystery in order to transcend it. The grace of faith draws Jew and Gentile alike into the Heart of the One, All Holy and Merciful God, Creator and Redeemer, with an invitation to believe and trust in his ultimate purposes of Love. The promise, however, is not simply one of personal joy and happiness from that day forward, but is a call to an all demanding discipleship: a human share in the costliness required for things to be set right and for sin and evil to be definitively overcome.

Such a discipleship is the awesome vocation of the Jewish people, consummated, Christians believe, in the life, death and resurrection of Jesus Christ: the Jew, Son of God and Son of Man. Gentile followers of Jesus are invited in turn to follow a similar shared path. May God, however, forgive people in history who have blamed the Jewish people for the sufferings of Jesus. This struggle will continue on until the Day the Lord, who will come at the time of his appointing.

Jean Lamb takes us to the heart of this mysterious ongoing struggle in her Stations of the Holocaust. The following meditations invite a personal commitment to share, in some small measure, in that cosmic battle. They are structured around the Book of Psalms: the prayer book of Jews and Christians alike. Firstly Jesus speaks, in the words of the psalms, of his own suffering and death and resurrection, all of which, as the Stations unfold, he was to undergo. Next the Jewish people, both before and after Christ, but especially in this instance the Holocaust victims, cry out in prayer and anguish, using words from the corporate prayers of the same Book of Psalms.

Let us then, in our turn, ask our God for a responsive heart in our journey through the Stations as he speaks to us through the combination of word and image.

Sister Mary Michael CHC

Station of the Holocaust I

Jesus is condemned to death:
the Jews are condemned to death

Visual Reflection

Jesus stands before his people, serene and melancholic as he faces the prospect of his own death. He stands before two sets of time. He is in his own time, yet turns to look forward to what will happen to his people in every century: especially culminating in the twentieth century. He has been condemned by Pontius Pilate whose hands sit limply on his knees as though giving up responsibility for what will happen to Jesus from now on (Luke 23.4). On his left stands one of the Jewish Scribes holding the Book of the Law which was used to condemn Jesus for blasphemy (John 19.7).

Below stands the Roman soldier who carried out the orders of his masters to varying degrees of brutality. Pilate and the Scribe stand under the classical architecture, spatially distanced from the people, with its perfect lines of raised steps denoting wealth and power. Jesus stands alone in the courtyard, a broken and troubled man: betrayed by one of his friends, and now deserted by all. He does not want to look at those who have condemned him, but stares ahead with pity at the impact this action will have upon future humanity.

There are three cauldrons of fire across the picture plane. One is behind the Roman soldier, another before the group of Nazi soldiers and the third to the far right corner of the sculpture, as though going off the edge and into the future. These cauldrons of fire are like markers in time, bringing the consequences of Jesus' condemnation right into our own century and further into the future.

The railway lines brush past the legs of the Centurion and travel on until they bring the herded European Jewish peoples into the very gates of death at Auschwitz. The people came, past the same fire of condemnation and brutality, to stand before the hateful scrutiny of Nazi soldiers before being swallowed by the gates of 'Arbeit macht frei'. Within weeks what remains of their flesh will be turned into a pitiful starving whimper, whose bodies are then burnt in purpose built ovens.

The head of Jesus is surrounded by wings of light, denoting both Jesus' holiness and the presence of the Father as he sees his son being taken away to death for our sins.

Jean Lamb

Meditation

'Behold the Man mighty to save, glorious in his strength, in meekness witnessing to truth.' (Father Gilbert Shaw)

The only wholly innocent one stands criminally condemned, accepting all. God, his Heavenly Father, calls him to this. In the depths of his heart Jesus can, at this point at least, confidently assert in the familiar words of the psalmist:

Jesus: 'Let the Lord judge the peoples. Vindicate me, Lord, according to my righteousness, according to my integrity, O most high' (Ps 7.8) 'Test me, Lord, and try me, examine my heart and my mind; for I have always been mindful of your unfailing love and have lived in reliance on your faithfulness' (Ps 26.2-3)

Under the protecting shelter of the Lord's Presence, the Shekinah, Jesus sets out on his walk of faithfulness, in obedience to his Father's will in order to secure the redemption of the world. Untold costliness lies ahead for him.

Such cost would not be his alone. It would impose itself inevitably, in some measure at least, on those nearest to him: his own mother, his close followers, his own Jewish people and those amongst the nations who later choose to follow him. Are we willing to go along too, whoever we are? Or do we prefer to screen our faces and pass by on the other side?

It is no comfortable pilgrimage. Before our eyes in this Station we see innocent, ordinary Jewish women, children and men suffering in the Holocaust, herded to their death. The human mind and heart cry out "Why! O why?". With the psalm writer, we also assail God in protest and yet, unaccountably, we will not let go of his assuring hope, trust and confidence.

Jews: 'Can a corrupt throne be allied with you - a throne that brings on misery by its decrees? The wicked band together against the righteous and condemn the innocent to death' (Ps 94.20-1) 'I know that the Lord secures justice for the poor and upholds the course of the needy. Surely the righteous will praise your name, and the upright will live in your presence' (Ps 140.12-13)

Without such a vestige of trust in God's incomprehensible providential care we could not even begin to set out on our own appointed journey in response to his call.

Sister Mary Michael CHC

Station of the Holocaust II

Jesus takes up his cross: the Jews are made to cart off their dead

Visual Reflection

The cross, blackened with sin, is placed upon the back of Jesus, his face contorted with pain for the concentration needed for the task (John 19.17). This is the beginning of the short journey from the centre of the city to the place of execution. Jesus, the one time carpenter, knows well the weight of wood. He lifts it with supreme strength and tries to carry it to its destination. So great is its weight that Jesus' feet make huge imprints on the ground.

He moves past the same houses and buildings as when he came into the City of Jerusalem, just a few days before, to celebrate the Passover with his disciples. He remembers the crowds which waved him on adoringly, shouting their adulations, "Hosanna to the Son of David" (John 12.13). Now the people look on silently, aghast that their Saviour and prophet is being herded to the hill of criminals, whilst others jeer and hurl abuse at him. One mother protectively wraps her arm around her young son, who is sprinkled by the tears and blood which pours out from Jesus' body as he walks past. A legacy of horror is being meted out to the next generation of witnesses to the death of Jesus.

Two thousand years later another set of guards cruelly watch the haggard occupants of the concentration camps collect their fellow pitiful specimens of humanity, who have died the previous night, and cart them to the open air furnaces of Birkenau, the offshoot of the Auschwitz concentration camp. The railway line just raises its iron profile above the hill of Jesus' walk to Golgotha. Like Jesus, for most inmates in the camps, death is the only way they can go.

Jean Lamb

Meditation

Burdened by his cross, Jesus sets out, purposefully clutching the instrument of his execution. His obedience is evident even in the face of death.

Despite the blood and sweat, Jesus trusts his Father implicitly. The psalms assure him:

> Jesus: 'I keep my eyes always on the Lord. With him at my right hand, I shall not be shaken. You make known to me the path of life' (Ps 16.8, 11) 'Let your face shine on your servant; save me in your unfailing love' (Ps 31.16)

And yet in this Station, the enigmatic mother and child suggest foreboding. The price of the world's salvation is a shared one for which we must play our part, since the blood of the Saviour falls upon each of us and upon our children's children.

The Holocaust victims are on a journey also: the dying hauling the dead along in the wake of Jesus who leads the way. See how the foot of the broken figure, unwillingly dragging the front cart along, touches a finger of Christ's hand as he grasps the cross. Two of the cross beams reach out beyond the frame of the carving into an infinity of time and space. The psalm writer also reaches out into that infinity through his words of prophecy;

> Jews: 'With cunning they conspire against your people; they plot against those you cherish. "Come" they say, "let us destroy them as a nation, so that Israel's name is remembered no more"' (Ps 83.3-4) 'Do all these evildoers know nothing? They devour my people as though eating bread; they never call on the Lord' (Ps 14.4)

Where are we in all this? Are we for or against? The soldier ponders the question too. How far are we responsible for the evils around us, simply because we do nothing?

Sister Mary Michael CHC

14

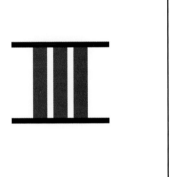

Station of the Holocaust III

Jesus falls for the first time:
a boy is shot

Visual Reflection

Inevitably Jesus falls under the weight of the cross. All of the lashes of the whip, the bleeding from the crown of thorns, the long hours of standing through the trials, first at Herod's Court and then with Pontius Pilate without any food or drink, have weakened him beyond the recognition of those who love him. Above all his heart is broken. All that he had given of himself to reveal the lost Kingdom of God to the people of Israel seems to have been inconsequential and forgotten.

Jesus claws the air for assistance, only to find the full weight of the cross fall upon him and crush him. Surrounded by a rowdy crowd of jeering onlookers he falls, alone.

The systematic destruction of the Jewish peoples by the Nazis did not just happen overnight. Hitler planned, with a demented logic, to progressively curtail the liberties which thousands of European Jews had enjoyed, particularly from the previous century. First professors, teachers and lawyers were not permitted to practice their profession. Then the Nazi's deported thousands of young men and women, forcing them to work in labour camps hundreds of miles away. They left behind their relatives who, without any means of support became increasingly destitute. Intimidation continued in public places and Synagogues were set alight. Shopkeepers were boycotted; customers blacklisted. Doctors were prohibited from practicing their profession, the sick were left to die. The Nazi's cordoned off whole sections of a city with high walls and barbed wire and all the Jewish inhabitants of the town were herded into ghettos where people shared rooms with up to ten others. There was no work and no means of earning money for food.

A small proportion of the inhabitants, the remaining young and fit, were permitted to leave the ghetto every day to work in the Aryan part of the city. Instead of wages, they might receive scraps of food, which were then distributed in the ghetto. The lack of food and resources meant thousands of the very young, orphans and the very old simply starved to death, begging on the streets. Disease was rampant. Finally ghettos were closed down by the Nazis. Stormtroopers would round everyone up into the town square whilst armed soldiers searched every block to hunt down anyone in hiding.

Sometimes people were given just five minutes to pack all their belongings and then made to stand all day in severe weather conditions until finally the long cattle trucks, completely enclosed, came to clear the town of its Jewish inhabitants.

All who resisted were shot. Here a young boy is shot as he resists being rounded up in the town square.

Jean Lamb

Meditation

Journeys are hazardous, this one above all. Even the Son of God stumbled and fell for a short while after starting off. Perhaps he did not watch his step since his mind and heart were elsewhere, already bearing the weight of our redemption. We dare not scoff, as some of the bystanders did. Already there is, in this Station, a fiery glow about the scene anticipating the Holocaust burnings. Jesus' massive hands display his anguish.

Despair, however, does not overwhelm him. This is just the start and he must pick himself up and move on. The Father decrees it; The Father enables it. So Jesus assures himself:

Jesus: 'The Lord makes firm the steps of the one who delights in him; though he may stumble, he will not fall, for the Lord upholds him with his hand' (Ps 37.23-24) 'Lord, I will wait for you; you will answer, Lord my God. For I said, "Do not let them gloat or exalt themselves over me when my feet slip"' (Ps 38.15-16)

The young Jewish boy, centuries later, didn't stop to think. He was simply reacting to the injustice around him and stood up to his persecutors. For that, he was shot. His 'fall' was fatal. The soldier made sure of that, despite whatever secret doubts he might have felt as he killed the boy. Orders after all, were orders:

Jews: 'Hear me, my God, as I voice my complaint; protect my life from the threat of the enemy. Hide me from the conspiracy of the wicked, from the plots of evildoers. They sharpen their tongues like swords and aim cruel words like deadly arrows. They shoot from ambush at the innocent; they shoot suddenly, without fear' (Ps 64.1-4) 'They close up their callous hearts, and their mouths speak with arrogance. They have tracked me down, they now surround me, with eyes alert, to throw me to the ground' (Ps 17.10-11)

What then, of ourselves? Whose orders count? Godless self interest? Or the promptings of enlightened conscience? When no doubt, inevitably, in our frailty, we fall into sin, do we still expect rehabilitation? Do we desire it and pray for it: for ourselves and for our neighbour also? To this Jesus invites us.

'Heal us, O Lord, and we shall be healed, redeem us speedily for your name's sake. Blessed are you: the Lord, the Healer of the sick of His people Israel'
(The Amidah, in the Jewish Prayer Book)

Sister Mary Michael CHC

18

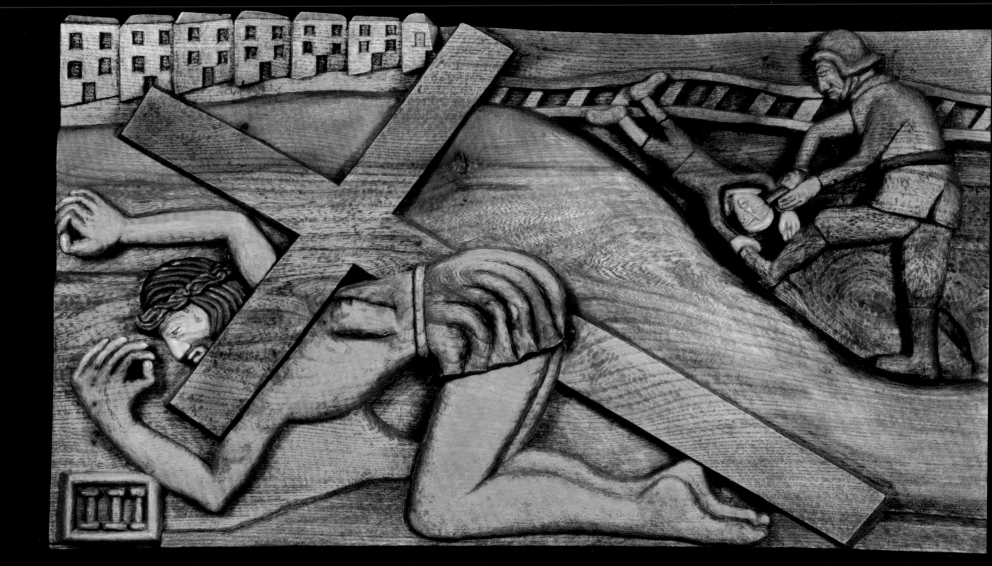

Station of the Holocaust IV

Jesus meets his mother for the last time: the Jewish mothers are separated from their children

Visual Reflection

The Gospels do not speak about this moment when perhaps Jesus was able to take a brief look at his mother for the last time, their hands brushing past each others bodies, saturated with sorrow. Every mother would move heaven and earth to touch their living child, to look deep into each others eyes for this last embrace before the terror to come. Here Jesus wants to give the best part of himself to his mother and allows his eyes to linger in tenderness for a fraction longer than the Roman soldiers would have permitted.

Mary is appalled, her chin resolutely set to see this scene of death through. She longs to touch the flesh which once lay nestled within her lap and Jesus responds, reaching out for her embrace. Mary bears the suffering of her son and wears her own crown of thorns. From her womb, a cross grows which will soon become the true Tree of Life on which her son will hang. For three years she has watched her son mature in his public ministry to become the majestic Son of Man, a new Son of Adam, in total obedience to the Father. Now the separation is to be final. This last embrace is what Jesus wanted to give his patient mother and what Mary needed to receive in the last minutes of her son's life.

When a new shipment of Jews arrived at a Nazi death camp, the soldiers ensured that families were separated. Men were split up from the women and children. Only the fit and healthy were selected to work. The old, the sick and the mothers with young children were immediately led to the gas chambers.

In this Station, the women with children have been rounded up at gun point and forced into the travelling gas lorries, where they would be killed. These gas lorries were prevalent at the beginning of the war and particularly used in the remote villages of Eastern Poland and White Russia. The Nazi's deceived the people by promising them that the lorries would take them on a short journey to a better camp. When the lorry was out of sight, perhaps in a wood, the driver would stop and fill the container with carbon monoxide. It would take as long as twenty to thirty minutes for people to die.

Above the head of Mary is another set of anonymous soldiers, symbolising the conflicts which continue today.

Jean Lamb

Meditation

As we travel through life towards the inevitability of death, when the days are dark and there seems no way out except through enduring ever greater waves of suffering, then we are to be drawn back through time, seeking the security of the beginning of things: the safe protective shelter of our mother's womb before the trauma of earthly life begun.

Those who, in God's providence, are snatched back from the grip of death tell us that at the moment when life seemed to be ebbing away, the experiences of their past life replayed before them. Jesus, in the fullness of his humanity would surely have experienced a similar flashback. Then suddenly, as tradition relates, Mary his mother appeared beside him on his way to Calvary. This would inevitably have been a brief encounter, but it was enough. His suffering was hers, insofar as she was enabled to bear it. Her pain in turn was acutely participated in by Jesus.

So it is still. Jesus has borne our griefs and carried our sorrows. Wondrously his mother Mary has been bequeathed to us by her son, through the person of St John, to be our mother too. Thus we too can justifiably relate to the prayers of the psalmist. These must have resonated often in the heart of Jesus, not least at the moment of such a poignant meeting:

> Jesus: 'From birth I was cast on you; from my mother's womb you have been my God. Do not be far from me, for trouble is near and there is no one to help' (Ps 22.10-11) 'Deliver me, my God, from the hand of the wicked, from the grasp of those who are evil and cruel. For you have been my hope, Sovereign Lord, my confidence since my youth. From my birth I have relied on you; you brought me forth from my mother's womb' (Ps 71.4-6)

Yet however comforting and mutually supportive this precious encounter may be, neither Jesus nor his mother are to hold onto it. Both must move on. Jesus to die in dereliction for the sins of the whole world. Mary to watch and look on powerlessly as the predicted suffering pierces deep into her own heart (Luke 2.35).

Already in this Station, Jesus is half turned towards the future. His left foot touches and moves towards the Holocaust mothers and their children as they are prodded and cajoled to their death. Above Mary's head the various effigies: symbols of humanity's ever recurring machismo are amassed. Will there ever be remission? The psalm writer does not give up hope but dimly perceives the salvation to be found in Jesus, the true Son of Man. Salvation for Jew and Gentile alike:

> Jews: '"They have greatly oppressed me from my youth" let Israel say; "they have greatly oppressed me from my youth, but they have not gained the victory over me"' (Ps 129.1-2) 'Return to us, God Almighty! Look down from heaven and see! Watch over this vine, the root your right hand has planted, the son you have raised up for yourself. Then we will not turn away from you; revive us, and we will call on your name. Restore us, Lord God Almighty; make your face shine on us, that we might be saved' (Ps 80.14-15,18 -19)

Salvation, however, for any of us, demands participation in a cross of suffering, as it did for Mary who carried the crucified one in her womb.

Sister Mary Michael CHC

Station of the Holocaust V

Simon of Cyrene helps Jesus with the cross: a mother helps her dying child before the pits

Visual Reflection

Jesus' body was weakening as he continued his journey up to Calvary. The Roman soldiers wanted to complete the execution as efficiently as possible, pressurised by the crowd roaring for blood. They realised that unless Jesus was given some assistance for at least part of the journey, Jesus was at risk of dying from exhaustion, leaving the crowd unsatisfied.

So Simon of Cyrene, a visitor from North Africa was press ganged into helping Jesus (Matthew 27.32). He takes the cross with tenderness and compassion, attempting to ease the burden for Jesus whose many open wounds chaff against the wood as Jesus carries the instrument of his own destruction.

Above the hills of Jerusalem in this Station lie the ploughed winter fields of twentieth century northern Europe which witness the wholesale slaughter of thousands of Jews. The relatively small mobile units of Einsatzgruppen soldiers were commissioned to enter an area, round up all the Jews at gunpoint, and herd them into the central square. They forced a select group of strong men to march into the neighbouring woods to dig vast pits. These pits had to have sufficient capacity to hold the Jewish inhabitants of the village. When the men had completed the task they were shot, falling into the pit they themselves had made. The rest of the village were marched up to the dugout pits, threatened to undress at gunpoint and told to line up so that as they were shot, they fell into the pit. The bodies were then covered with lime to hasten decomposition.

Here a mother holds her dying child before she too will be shot. She stands at the end of the ploughed field, situated above the back of Jesus. 'Ploughmen have ploughed my back and made their furrows long' (Psalm 129.3).

Jean Lamb

Meditation

Here we see Jesus striving to continue on his way, moving relentlessly onwards towards his death. He is between different times: both on the road to Golgotha and pressing along with his suffering peoples until the end of time. Though he becomes glorified and immortal in his resurrection, at this point he has to suffer, just as humanity will suffer.

Life's journey for each of us is often lonesome. Although we seek mutual support in community, it is hard to find love and to love others. Simon of Cyrene was going his own way when coerced into carrying the cross of Jesus. Was he resentful, a reluctant sharer in a stranger's fate?

As for Jesus, he inevitably turned to his heavenly Father for help in his extreme need, knowing that he would be at hand. Yet in this moment, help came to him through human agency, through an act of compassion by a complete stranger who was not even a fellow Jew:

Jesus: 'My God, in his steadfast love will meet me; God will go before me' (Ps 59.10) 'But as for me, I am poor and needy; come quickly to me, O God. You are my help and my deliverer; Lord do not delay' (Ps 70.5)

All the same, the brutality of human depravity and consequent suffering imposed on by others in the centuries that follow Calvary overwhelm us. How can we believe in a merciful, all powerful God in a world of suffering? We do not have Simon of Cyrene to assist us. Jesus alone has the power to bear it all and uphold us.

Before us carved in wood, we see the figure of a mother carrying her dying child. She stands there starkly, arms outstretched. She looks down to the pit which soon will be her own grave. The contrast and comparisons of images in this Station reveal that the evils done to God's people are evils shared in by Jesus, himself a Jew. Small wonder that his suffering ones, the Holocaust victims, cry out for redress:

Jews: 'You have rejected us, God, and burst upon us; you have been angry - now restore us! Save us and help us with your right hand, that those you love may be delivered. Is it not you, God, you who have now rejected us? Give us aid against the enemy, for human help is worthless' (Ps 60.1,5,10,11)

Small wonder that we too are called upon to acknowledge our sins of indifference and inertness and to take up our personal cross of shared involvement, definitively.

Sister Mary Michael CHC

VI

Station of the Holocaust VI
Veronica wipes the face of Jesus: Jesus sees the faces of the suffering children

Visual Reflection

There is an ancient tradition that a woman in the crowds, after witnessing Jesus' suffering, took out her cloth to wipe the sweat and blood from his head as he staggered towards his destination. The tradition also states that as she retrieved the cloth, she saw the actual face of Jesus imprinted into the very fabric of the cloth. It is plausible that Jesus' face would have burned with energy as he struggled on towards his death. If we recognise this, then perhaps Veronica's compassionate act reveals something profoundly true. When we perform a loving act for others, others can see God in us.

In this Station, it is not Jesus' face that we see imprinted in Veronica's cloth, but Jesus foresees the suffering humanity which will come after him. More precisely, these are the faces of the millions of children who were tortured and starved to death during the Nazi regime, and represent the children who will continue to suffer until the end of time. Their faces are grey and ashen after weeks without food, weakened under conditions of slavery in the camps. They are imprisoned, mute and dazed. In contrast Jesus is still strong enough to hold himself. In this moment, Jesus is not praying so much for himself as for those who will come after him.

The name Veronica means 'true likeness'. Her vocation is to bear the image of the true likeness of God deeply in her heart forever. She represents all those who continue to wait for Jesus in poverty, chastity and obedience, until his return.

The Nazi boots hover above the head of Veronica as they point their guns towards the children. The worst atrocity was committed in the camps when the gas chambers became too full. Although they were able to hold 2000 victims at a time, the Nazi officials insisted on killing thousands more.

Their solution was to make pyres in the open grounds surrounding Birkenau where queues of children were formed to be thrown into the flames alive.

Jean Lamb

Meditation

'Our Father, our King! Have compassion upon us, on our children and on our infants; act, for the sake of those who went through fire and water for the sanctification of your name.'
(Petition used on days of Penitence, Jewish Prayer Book)

Journeys require stopping places for refreshment. The boxer in the ring has brief moments of respite to regain energy and be revived for the next round. Veronica, with womanly compassion braved the brawling mob and the hardened authorities. She devoutly follows Jesus towards his crucifixion, to wipe the blood and sweat from his face and temporarily ease his discomfort. Great was her reward.

Humanity, originally made in the image of God (Genesis 1.26-27), tarnished that image through sin. Now Jesus momentarily restores it to Veronica, on the cloth she had proffered him, in foretaste of what would be brought about through his death and resurrection. Veronica herself personifies all who draw near to God in the deeper levels of prayer, all who desire his beauty, the definitive restitution of creation and the ultimate coming of the Kingdom:

> Veronica: "One thing I ask from the Lord, this only do I seek: that I may dwell in the house of the Lord all the days of my life, to gaze on the beauty of the Lord. Your face, Lord, I will seek. Do not hide your face from me" (Ps 27.4,8,9)

But in the Station before us the imprinted image is not one of comfort, especially for Jesus. Not only is the divine image hidden beneath Jesus' own suffering face, it reveals the distorted faces of innocent victims in the future. Veronica herself already perceives this. Her face reveals not only the inexpressible bliss of communion with God but also the deep suffering that is inevitably entailed in such a privilege. Once more it is the voice of the psalmist who allows us to share something of the anguished questionings of the Jewish people:

> Jews: 'O God, why have you rejected us forever? Why does your anger smoulder against the sheep of your pasture?' (Ps 74.1) 'May the Lord answer you when you are in distress; May the name of the God of Jacob protect you. May he remember all your sacrifices and accept your burnt offerings' (Ps 20.1,3) You answer us with awesome and righteous deeds, God our Saviour' (Ps 65.5)

Whatever sufferings might still lie ahead, for Jesus as for ourselves, faith and hope assure us that God reigns, and we one day will reign with him.

Sister Mary Michael CHC

Station of the Holocaust VII

Jesus falls for the second time:
the Jews are rounded up in the ghetto

Visual Reflection

Again the weight of the cross takes its toll on Jesus and he finds himself on the ground, crushed by the wood of the tree. As a young man he could have held the weight of the wood, but here the mental torture is as fierce as the physical, and he falls, appalled at the prospect of his own death. On the ground, Jesus' eyes are half closed in exhaustion. No one can help him now. No one dare help him now. His right arm flails around in the air, reaching out for the help which has been denied him. In so doing it crosses the boundaries of time and space to provide assistance to those who continue to call upon the name of Jesus, a derivative of the Jewish name Joshua, which means Saviour.

Jesus falls on the hill of Jerusalem but his body is stretched out upon a modern road, bordered by huge housing blocks to form the edge of the ghetto. His right arm calls for assistance in one time zone, but provides assistance in another time zone, as it seems to shield the rounded up Jews from the firing power of the Nazis. Here in the top left hand corner we see the ghetto enclosure: lorries have been brought in to carry the people to the nearest railway station so that they can be transported to a death camp. Inside the open lorry is a tiny nativity, an image of the beginning of life.

Was God the Father remembering how he placed his son into the womb of Mary and provided protection for them through Joseph? The indescribable discomfort of Jesus, falling for the second time under the weight of the cross, is contrasted with the soft beauty which he received at the hands of his young mother.

Even in the ghetto, the drive for life continued. Countless babies were conceived and born in terrible circumstances. Amongst the houses of the ghetto, tunnels were made, cellars concealed and roof spaces boarded over to create hiding places for families seeking refuge from the Nazi thugs. Families with young children were at risk within such hiding places as if the child were to cry, their location would be revealed. Often, the child was smothered by its own parents. 'A voice is heard in Ramah, weeping and great mourning, Rachel weeping for her children and refusing to be comforted, because they are no more' (Jeremiah 31.15 in Matthew 2.18).

Jean Lamb

33

Meditation

'Have mercy, O Lord our God, on Israel your people. Speedily relieve us from all our troubles. Let us not be in need of the gifts of men, but only of your helping hand, which is full, open, holy and ample.' (Grace after Meals on Purim, Jewish Prayer Book)

Jesus falls again, worse than before, flat on the ground. The scene is dark and he is utterly alone, for in his damaged half conscious state even the frenzied crowd about him has melted into oblivion. Of the people, no one was with him. He looked for human aid but found none. Deep fear of his own impending fate thrust him down, for after all he was human through and through, though Son of God.

More than that, a sudden awareness of the anguish yet to be endured by those he had come to save pierced his very being. His own people especially, since they unwittingly shared in his vocation, were destined to have their ongoing part in his redemptive suffering, throughout the ages. Perhaps that was almost more than he could then bear.

Thus, we see his own holy right hand spread out in outrage, and in so doing he spiritually draws all the future anguish back down into himself. Since he does only what God the Father wills for him, Jesus looks to him for the enabling:

Jesus: 'When I was in distress, I sought the Lord; at night I stretched out untiring hands, and I would not be comforted' (Ps 77.2) 'Truly he is my rock and my salvation; he is my fortress, I shall not be shaken. My salvation and my honour depend on God; he is my mighty rock, my refuge' (Ps 62.5-7)
'In the course of my life he broke my strength; he cut short my days' (Ps 102.23)

It is not possible for us to be mere onlookers in this scene. It profoundly moves us. We have to go on saying our 'yes' to whatever God may be asking of us, in order that we may help to hasten on the Day of the Lord, and ease the burden of those whose suffering far exceeds our own. It is a call both to profound prayer and intercession as well as service to a ministry of encouragement for the renewal of hope. This must motivate us to challenge all forms of religious and racial hatred. Most assuredly, the arm and hand of our Lord is not so shortened that it cannot help.

Jews: 'They pour out arrogant words; all the evildoers are full of boasting. They crush your people, Lord; they oppress your inheritance' (Ps 94.4-5) 'Arise, Lord! Lift up your hand, O God. Do not forget the helpless' (Ps 10.12) 'You who seek God, may your hearts live! The Lord hears the needy and does not despise his captive people' (Ps 69.32-33)

Sister Mary Michael CHC

Station of the Holocaust VIII
The weeping women of Jerusalem: woman fleeing with her children: children punished in the death camps

Visual Reflection

Jesus takes up his cross again. He has not only been followed by his mother, but by many other women who seem to have no fear of the Roman soldiers. Seeing Jesus pass by, both young and old stop to weep and wail loudly at the fate of their Saviour, the one who was meant to rescue Israel from the Romans. He healed their children (Mark 7.25,26,30) and brought others back to life (Mark 5.22,23,41).

A wise old woman stands at the foot of the carried cross, her face full of anguish as she looks squarely at the fate of Jesus. She has brought her grand daughter. This little girl, together with her pregnant mother actually stand on the end of the cross, for it is from their generation onwards that the renewed suffering of the Jewish peoples begin, with the fall of the second Temple 70 AD. It is for these that Jesus forewarns that no tears are necessary. Rather tears should be shed for the succeeding generations of women who will metaphorically carry his cross (Luke 23.27-31).

As Jesus tucks his arm over the cross, his body is silhouetted by the serrated lines of the railway which mark the twentieth century time zone, diagonally cut across the picture plane. Our eyes are drawn, following the track to the concentration camps where row upon row of improvised gallows perform their task on the young girls and boys, separated from their parents. As the result of such brutality, these children became feral in order to survive inhuman conditions without the protection of their mothers and fathers. They have been hung for transgressing Nazi boundaries: for stealing a slice of bread or being absent for roll call. Their rigid bodies hang for days, warnings to other children not to imitate any expression of freedom whilst the water filled ploughed fields bare witness to their suffering. A Nazi Guard stands, watching over the helpless abandoned children.

His insignia represents succeeding generations of soldiers throughout the world who blindly follow the orders of dictators, clerics and unelected governments.

In the foreground, a Jewish woman carries her tiny baby and leads her terrified young children. She does not know where to flee. The girl's doll is naked and limp as soon she will be.

Jean Lamb

Meditation

Could these appalling extermination camps have been allowed by God? Only God's severe mercy has the power to defeat evil irrevocably. He took his creation upon himself uncompromisingly, in the humanity of his son, to become the unspeakable price to definitely annihilate all powers of darkness. Thus he, Jesus, is with us all in the ensuing conflict until the end of time.

That is why, in this Station, Jesus appears to have changed direction, no longer merely pressing on towards his own Passion but already moving forwards to an ongoing future of participated suffering. The grieving women of Jerusalem weep for him and he in turn weeps not only for them, but for their children's children through the generations. Things would get worse before the cosmic battle would come to an end, historically speaking. Jesus and the weeping mothers cry out alike to the Lord:

> Jesus and the women of Jerusalem: 'Indignation grips me because of the wicked, you have forsaken your law. Streams of tears flow from my eyes, for your law is not obeyed' (Ps 119.53,136) 'Save your people and bless your inheritance; be their shepherd and carry them for ever' (Ps 28.9)

Only with the sacrificial support of their Shepherd Lord will the remnant of his people pull through.

Jesus, with his body and with his cross, enfolds the stunned and fearful mother and her children. The mother stands on his very foot since they travel on together. Likewise the Jerusalem women and child stand at the foot of his cross: the cross which stretches out in all its parts beyond the confines of the carving. It is endless. The railway line too traverses all time. The enigmatic God of both severity and goodness alone can break the power of sin in which all humanity in every epoch is implicated. In the horror of the Holocaust the people pray:

> Jews: 'You, Lord, will keep the needy safe and will protect us for ever from the wicked, who strut about when what is vile is honoured by the human race' (Ps 12.7-8) 'Why, Lord, do you stand far off? Why do you hide yourself in times of trouble? Break the arm of the wicked man; call the evildoer to account for his wickedness that would not otherwise be found out' (Ps 10.1,15)

Devout and believing Jews and Christians alike yearn for a final return from exile into the promised Kingdom of God's justice, righteousness, peace and love, with the definitive return of the promised Messiah. Dare we thus in penitence pray together:

> 'O you who are One Lord, and your Name One, have mercy upon us all who are called by your Name, and make us more and more one in you. O King of Righteousness and peace, gather us more and more into your kingdom, and make us both, Gentile and Jew, visibly and invisibly one in yourself. Amen'

Sister Mary Michael CHC

Station of the Holocaust IX

Jesus falls for the third time:
Jewish victims of experimentation in
vats of freezing water

Visual Reflection

Jesus finally has no more strength for the journey. He slumps to the ground in misery and exhaustion, his swollen eyes clamped shut. The Roman soldiers had brutally ensured that Jesus' body was lashed, scourged and bruised and this time Jesus could not go on. His hands curl around his beaten head as though he were wanting to cradle a wounded child, but the crown of thorns digs deeper into his flesh as he falls.

A young man steps forward to grab the cross before it falls back onto Jesus' body. He looks down at Jesus, the condemned man who is to die, with shock and horror. Jesus' brokenness reminds the man of his own brokenness and vulnerability. The cross he holds for Jesus is upside down. This is a symbol that the world Jesus came to save is itself upside down, full of brokenness and pain. Profoundly, restoration is only possible through the powerful intervention of God.

In the background, behind the vast stretch of what looks like the open sea, we are taken to the chaos of life in a Nazi death camp. Out of view, the carefully hand picked victims, who had been paraded with malicious intent before the white coated Nazi doctors became the subject of brutal experimentation. With clinical precision each victim was weighed and dressed, replicating the uniform which the Luftwaffe wore on their bombing missions over London. The Nazi doctors were curious to find out how long a person could live in the freezing temperatures of the North Sea, were their plane to be shot down. The victims were either submerged until they lost consciousness and died, or until they lost consciousness and were revived through forced resuscitation of human bodily contact. Animal fur was wrapped around the semi conscious victims after they were removed from the tanks.

Once recovered, the experiment would be repeated. All their reactions were measured and monitored in meticulous detail, which included photographic evidence.

Their findings were the same as what common sense would have informed any sensible State: one which was not itself upside down.

Jean Lamb

Meditation

A third fall for Jesus who anticipates his death. Sooner or later we shall arrive at the same place. The anonymous Onlooker is Everyman: from Adam, naked in Paradise, falling into sin and shame, right up to the Second Adam, Jesus, himself returning at the end of time in the glory of creation renewed with Paradise unendingly regained.

Although the cross hides the Onlookers' nakedness, it does not hide the profound sadness and questioning on his face. "Have I a part in this: Am I to blame?" None of us can in fact escape our involvement in the totality of the world's sinfulness. It would be preferable in our eyes to turn away and refuse to participate, but we cannot. Jesus himself, in the Garden of Gethsemane, begged his Father to take the cup of suffering away from him if it were possible, but ultimately submitted.

Jesus: 'Look on me and answer, Lord my God. Give light to my eyes, or I will sleep in death' (Ps 13.3) 'Answer me when I call to you, my righteous God. Give me relief from my distress; have mercy on me and hear my prayer. The Lord hears when I call to him. In peace I will lie down and sleep, for you alone, Lord, make me dwell in safety' (Ps 4.1,3,8)

Everyman, however, must pass through the waters, the stream of death and life. This is first achieved in symbol: the Red Sea for the Hebrew people and the River Jordan of Baptism for the Christian. The blue stream of water at the centre of this Station flows transparently through the body of the Onlooker, almost up to the neck. The victims of Nazi experimentation are likewise deeply immersed in icy waters, with no escape. Agonisingly, God seems to have a part in it all, if only by allowing it to happen.

Yet who, without God's intervention, could hope to reach the promised other side?

Jews: 'If the Lord had not been on our side - let Israel say - if the Lord had not been on our side, when people attacked us, they would have swallowed us alive when their anger flared against us' (Ps 124.1-3) 'For you, God, tested us; and laid burdens on our backs. We went through fire and water, but you brought us to a place of abundance' (Ps 66.10,11,12)

Nevertheless, even at this point Jesus is not at his destination. He must drag himself up and travel on to the bitter end. The world and its people likewise must struggle on. Through this, let us support one another, ease each other's burdens and uphold one another in prayer.

Sister Mary Michael CHC

42

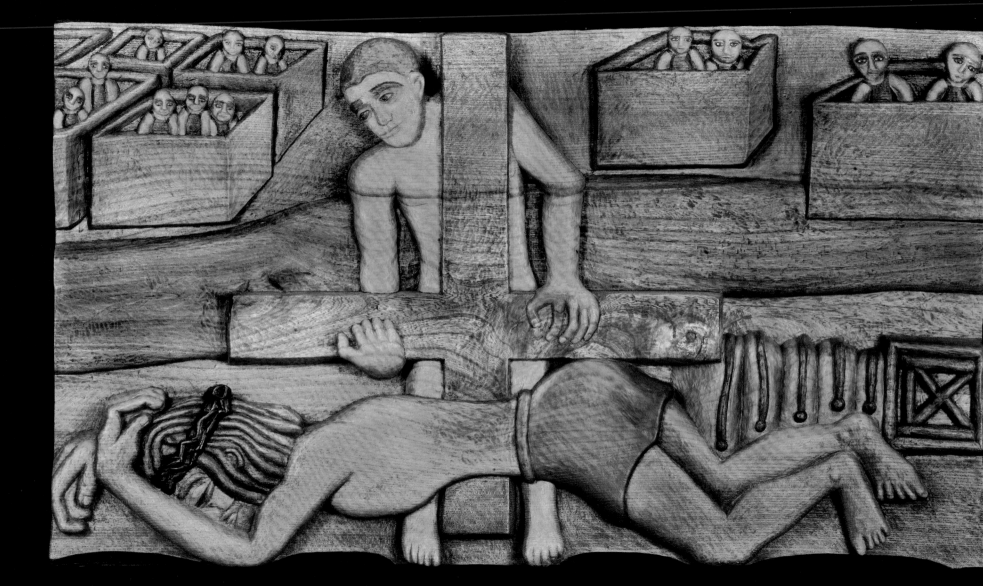

Station of the Holocaust X

Jesus is disrobed:
the destruction of all flesh

Visual Reflection

In the final act before crucifixion, prisoners were stripped of their clothes. Surely the greatest punishment next to death is to suffer shame. The soldiers forcibly uncovered Jesus' most private, intimate parts, to the jeering onlookers. Here Jesus stands unashamed, opening his broken blooded arms out to greet the whole world. His arms are elongated with the desire to hold the true prisoners of the world in his embrace. His broken welcome invites us all to share in his sufferings, to notice the injustice and to apply his example of vulnerable love to every situation of oppression in our world.

The words 'Behold the Man' are written upon the cross beam of the executioner's tree. Jesus is the True Man of the world. He has no sin within his body, yet his body bears every sin ever committed by every human being who has lived and will live. For us he has revealed his true self, the second Adam correcting the sin and taking on the punishment of the first (2 Corinthians 5.21).

In the top right hand corner we see an angel of God chasing Adam and Eve out of the Garden of Eden with a sword (Genesis 1.27,28,31). To the left of the picture a burnt tree stands in the middle of what has become a desert. To the right is the massive and fierce sun which explodes with nuclear energy. Its rays attack Jesus through the heat of the day, as he suffers on the cross, before its erratic energy is turned to darkness for three hours, from noon (Matthew 27.45). Below, we see the tangled mass of steel and wood, once the pride of Europe: the railway. These steel tracks, built in the nineteenth century are a symbol of the way in which the Industrial Revolution irrevocably transformed the environment, which itself will be destroyed through climate change.

The Nazis deliberately removed people's clothing and all of their personal possessions to accentuate their vulnerability. When the Jewish captives arrived at the camps, they were forced to strip off all their clothes and parade in front of Gestapo Inspectors. Anyone who was ill, injured or old were taken straight to the gas chambers. The healthy were selected for special tasks such as heavy manual work, sewing or sorting the clothes of the victims. Some camps were dedicated to the Nazi war effort and the Jewish inmates were expected to make armaments. The most beautiful young, teenage virgins were taken as prostitutes. Their rapes might last days or weeks, but if they became pregnant they were sent to the gas chambers. Hitler had prohibited all sexual relations between Aryan Germans and Jews but in the camps, the soldiers had their own rules.

The robe which was taken off Jesus was seamless (John 19.23). Here a Jewish prayer robe parts to reveal the true Son of Man, who once stood naked in the River Jordan before John at his Baptism. The blue stripes of the robe are a reminder of the flow of prayer between earth and heaven continuing incessantly through the last six hours of Jesus' life.

All who were not useful to the Nazi regime were destroyed, as were so many families who were piled high, like rubbish.

Jean Lamb

Meditation

The stripping away of outward protectiveness will come to us all, before the end. Even Jesus, the incarnate Christ, in his total innocence was not exempt. Piety itself was torn from him and there was now nothing to shelter him from the blasphemies of his mocking enemies: "Where, then, is your God?"

Naked but without shame and displaying the full perfection of his human form, despite its bruised brokenness, Jesus presents himself resolutely to our gaze. Dare we respond by fixing our eyes on him?

While still totally depending on his Father, nevertheless Jesus knows full well how things are. What is still to come will be so abhorrent that people could turn their backs on God forever. Would he be responsible for that?

> Jesus: 'But I am a worm and not a man, scorned by everyone, despised by the people. All who see me mock me; they hurl insults, shaking their heads. All my bones are on display; people stare and gloat over me. They divide my clothes among them and cast lots for my garment' (Ps 22.6-7,17-18) 'Lord, the Lord Almighty, may those who hope in you not be disgraced because of me; God of Israel, may those who seek you not be put to shame because of me. For I endure scorn for your sake, and shame covers my face. I am a foreigner to my own family, a stranger to my own mother's children' (Ps 69.6-8)

Yet Jesus here is cosmic in dimension, he is truly the Son of Man (Mark 10.45), the Sinless One. Past, present and future meet in his full self exposure. Adam and Eve are driven from Paradise marking the first sin of divisiveness between the sexes: 'Your desire will be for your husband and he will rule over you' (Genesis 3.16). In the top right corner we see Eve's shock and horror as the angel's sword brushes against her breasts.

Just below the expulsion scene, rape is depicted in all its stark crudity. All around are the signs of murder, death and violence. The soldier muses: "Do I shoot or do I let it be?" The figures on the left lie dead beneath the uprooted Tree of Life. All the comforting protections of family and communal life are disintegrating. Even the sun is darkened, threateningly.

The totality of evil throughout the ages is concentrated here in the death of Jesus, the sinless Son of God. Yet in this moment, life itself draws near. His death will ultimately lead to the final overthrow of evil and the dawn of unending life. This restoration will not happen yet. God's people still cry out in prayer and we with them:

> Jews: 'You have rejected us, God. You have shown your people desperate times. But for those who fear you, you have raised a banner to be unfurled against the bow. Save us and help us with your right hand, that those you love may be delivered' (Ps 60.1,3-5) 'Have mercy on us, Lord, have mercy on us, for we have endured no end of contempt' (Ps 123.3) 'Pour out your wrath on the nations that do not acknowledge you, on the kingdoms that do not call on your name; for they have devoured Jacob and devastated his homeland. Do not hold against us the sins of past generations; may your mercy come quickly to meet us, for we are in desperate need' (Ps 79.6-8)

Sister Mary Michael CHC

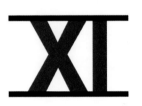

Station of the Holocaust XI
The crucifixion of Jesus:
the children are thrown into open fires

Visual Reflections

The moment of crucifixion arrives. Jesus is made to stretch out his body on the cross to allow the Roman soldiers to pin his hands and his feet onto the wooden beams. He screams out with pain, together with the other two prisoners. Their sounds form a harrowing chorus roar which stretches across the Kidron Valley into the heart of Jerusalem. Jesus' face is no longer placid, but takes on the shape of a monster, hardly human, as the nails beat their sharp points deep into the wood: his flesh between. His hands are battered to a pulp of blood. The hammers sculpt their rivers of pain around his head, where the sign board mocks 'INRI': shorthand for Jesus of Nazareth the King of the Jews. So deep are the furrows describing his pain, that the chisel has gone through the wood of the Station.

Jesus is the Lamb of God who takes away the sin of the world (John 1.29). In the Synoptic Gospels, Jesus eats the Passover with his disciples before his betrayal and arrest. There Jesus breaks the Unleavened Bread of haste at the beginning of the meal. Then the roasted lamb is eaten. In the ritualised slaughter of the lamb, the beast is strung upside down, its throat slit open, and as it dies, its blood is poured into bowls to be used for the ceremony of Passover (Exodus 12.7). At the beginning of the Passover meal Jesus took the cup of wine (Luke 22.18) and gave it to his disciples to drink, thereby remembering the first Covenant God made with his people. On the Passover night, before the journey from Egypt to the Sinai desert, the blood of the first born one year old lamb was daubed on the lintels of the door posts to protect the people of Israel's first born son from the destroyer (Exodus 12.23).

The Gospel of John however takes the moment of the Passover to be the crucifixion of Jesus on the cross, so that he bears the wrath of God. Jesus therefore becomes the Passover Lamb whose spilt blood is poured out to take away the sins of his people Israel and all the peoples of the world.

In the Station, Jesus' body is smeared with blood from such a slaughtered lamb. His crown of thorns is like the burnt bundle of wood on which Abraham prepared to offer his own son as a sweet smelling oblation to God. There are set drops of incense grains placed into the burnt wood, a sign of the offering that God continues to ask of his people.

The place where Jesus and the two criminals were crucified was called the Place of the Scull, Golgotha: the regular site of execution. Placed outside the walls of Jerusalem, this bare rock was once, so legend has it, the site of the beautiful Garden of Eden. After the fall of Adam and Eve, sin and death entered the world (Genesis 3). Their first born son Cain, murdered his brother Abel out of jealousy. So Adam's skull is the tinderbox which sets light to the innocent victims of the Jewish Holocaust, first fanned into a living hell by the ubiquitous jealousy of Cain and then all other despots after him, culminating in Hitler in the twentieth century.

Each perfect child of God who has stood before the flames of one man's inhuman vision becomes part of the anonymous sacrifice which is given the name Holocaust, meaning a burnt offering.

Jean Lamb

Meditation

Adoni Rahem: Lord Have Mercy

The most terrible moment of all? The living Jesus is nailed to the cross, bearing unimaginable pain. It is a moment of unsurpassable blasphemy and yet in his last agony he murmurs: "Father, forgive them for they do not know what they are doing" (Luke 23.34). Love dies, out of love for humankind.

But love cannot ultimately die. For true love is stronger than death, fiercer than even the Holocaust fires. Jesus, here is depicted as radically alone, except for the future dead whose fate he is soon to share. His left hand touches them, not in protection but in agonised fellowship. Already he anticipates his descent into hell, already he senses total abandonment: "My God, my God, why have you forsaken me?" (Matthew 27.46).

> Jesus: 'Do not hide your face from me, do not turn your servant away in anger; you have been my helper. Do not reject me or forsake me, God my Saviour' (Ps 27.9) 'I am worn out calling for help; my throat is parched. My eyes fail, looking for my God' (Ps 69.3) 'My mouth is dried up like a potsherd, and my tongue sticks to the roof of my mouth; you lay me in the dust of death' (Ps 22.15)

Fulfilling the Father's will actually demands all this: God abandoning his Son on the cross in the seeming absence of his presence. Bearing the price of sin requires it and only in this way can humankind find fellowship again with God. We may weep at the sight of his mangled body, parched tongue and contorted features. Is it not too much? We even dare to ask if we might help to ease the burden.

Creation too is void. The blood red fields are parched. The rock above is barren and sharp, the consequence of the world's wickedness.

The Holocaust victims too felt cruelly abandoned at this point, as the psalmist predicted:

> Jews: 'Will the Lord reject for ever? Will he never show his favour again? Has his unfailing love vanished for ever? Has his promise failed for all time? Has God forgotten to be merciful? Has he in his anger withheld his compassion?' (Ps 77.7-9) 'They have left the dead bodies of your servants as food for the birds of the sky, the flesh of your own people for the animals of the wild. They have poured out blood like water all around Jerusalem, and there is no one to bury the dead' (Ps 79.2-3)

The mocking title 'King of the Jews' is profoundly more true than those who chose to set it could ever have imagined. Vindication however, has yet to come in its fullness.

Sister Mary Michael CHC

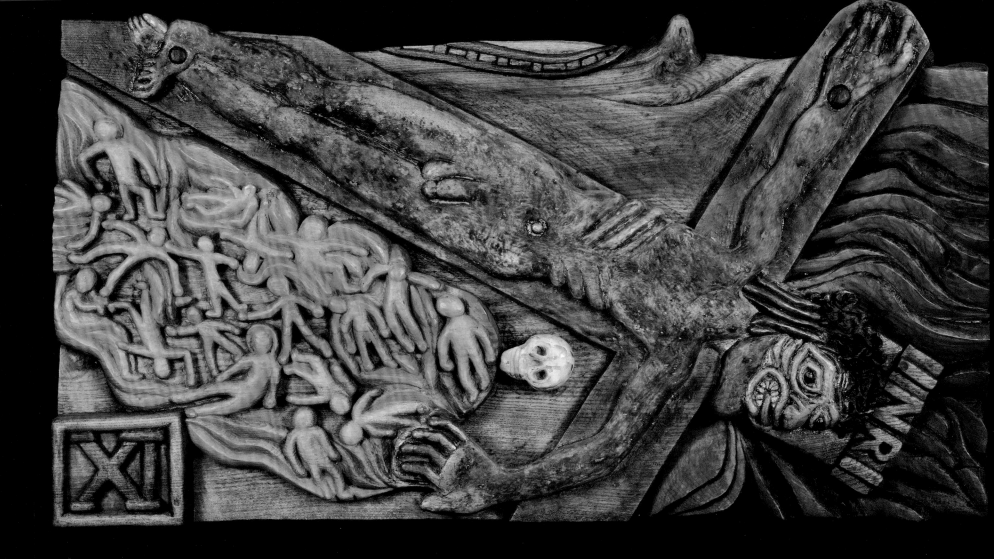

Station of the Holocaust XII

Jesus dies for the whole world:
the Jews bless one another before the
ovens of Auschwitz

Visual Reflection

From 12 noon until 3pm, the time it took for Jesus to die, the sun was in eclipse (Matthew 27.45). Now Jesus, the Light of the World, was extinguished at the same time as the whole world plunged into darkness. His arms are stretched out on a cross which has no end, symbolising that Jesus died for the whole world. Carved at the top of the cross is written σωτήρ, Saviour, in Greek which is the language of the original New Testament. Braided on Jesus' head is a red and green crown of thorns, which symbolises the green shoots of the Tree of Life.

Jesus looks down from the cross towards the Penitent Thief, giving assurance that he too will share eternity with him (Luke 23.42,43). They are both naked, a reference not only to their physical nakedness but also a symbol of the time in the Garden of Eden when mankind's nakedness was a sign of their union with God. In contrast, the Impenitent Thief is dressed as a soldier who wears the insignia of totalitarian regimes which have and are still seeking world domination. He will not join Jesus in paradise when he dies.

To the left of Jesus are two fir trees. These stand as witnesses to the desecration of humanity across Northern Europe, darkly echoing the two Southern Olive Trees which stood in the Temple of God (Zechariah 4.14). When Jesus dies, there is an earthquake and the Veil of the Temple is torn in two. Jesus' death ends the separation between priest and people in the Holy of Holies (Matthew 27.50-1), so the whole world becomes an operative place of sanctification for the Blood of the Lamb. The fir tree is emblematic of the lands which bore witness to the greatest suffering of the Holocaust: Germany, Poland, Lithuania, White Russia. Like their predecessors in Eden, these trees stand as witnesses in the open air, which has once again become the Temple of the Lord.

Next to the trees is the Auschwitz Crematorium and many other Nazi Crematoriums, built to consume Jewish, critical and fringe humanity, gassed in vast underground vaults before their bodies were burned. Now knowing their fate, the Jewish mothers and fathers bless each other, holding their little children as they are directed relentlessly towards the locked doors of their enclosure (Ps 44.1).

Above their head flows the remnants of a Jewish prayer robe, whose distinctive blue stripes are reminiscent of the monstrous railway as it undulates gently above the terrible scene to form an arch of light with a stole of blessing.

Jean Lamb

Meditation

Jesus stretches out his hand on a cross which has no end. Nothing can escape or be hidden from this cosmic cataclysm, not even our own paltry sinfulness. Though the sun eclipsed when Jesus was crucified there is now nothing hidden that shall not be revealed (Luke 8.17). Nevertheless, the choice of repentance is ours. We have to either accept redemption by trusting God and his purposes or choose to turn away from him. With whom do we identify: the 'good thief' or the 'other one'?

Jesus is in the throes of death. In his agony he questions: "Will my Heavenly Father not rescue me?"

Jesus: 'Lord, how many are my foes! How many rise up against me! Many are saying of me, "God will not deliver him' (Ps 3.1-2) 'I hate those you cling to worthless idols; as for me, I trust in the Lord. Be merciful to me, Lord, for I am in distress; my eyes grow weak with sorrow, my soul and body with grief. My life is consumed by anguish and my years by groaning; my strength fails because of my affliction, and my bones grow weak. Because of all my enemies, I am the utter contempt of my neighbours and an object of dread to my closest friends - those who see me on the street flee from me. I am forgotten as though I were dead; I have become like broken pottery' (Ps 31.6, 9-12)

The two thieves, battling in the same struggle between good and evil, symbolise the tearing apart of Jesus' whole being in the conflict. The two trees of witness look on throughout history, until the world's end. They were there at Auschwitz and Birkenau, watching innocence being swallowed up in an abyss of evil: a seemingly unending hell of fire. The prayer shawl and stole of Judeo Christian piety seems to overshadow the doomed people.

Yet God's people do not fall into utter despair. Some at least, will not let go of their God, who has shown his faithfulness in history. The stench from the ovens will not carry on forever:

Jews: 'In God we make our boast all day long, and we will praise your name for ever. But now you have rejected and humbled us. You gave us up to be devoured like sheep and have scattered us among the nations. You sold your people for a pittance, gaining nothing from their sale. You have made us a byword among the nations; the peoples shake their heads at us' (Ps 44.8, 9,11,12,14) 'But you remain the same, and your years will never end. The children of your servants will live in your presence; their descendants will be established before you' (Ps 102.27-28) 'For the Lord will not reject his people; he will never forsake his inheritance' (Ps 94.14)

Can we, Gentile or Jew, as we stand before this Station and as we look out upon our troubled world sense our own share in the guilt of it all? Can we truly and meaningfully embrace that same hope of God's pledged redemption available to us all, which will save us from all that is evil? Lord we do believe, please help our unbelief.

Sister Mary Michael CHC

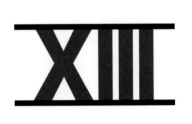

Station of the Holocaust XIII
The deposition of Jesus from the cross: the Jews are lined up to be shot and to fall into pits

Jesus dies on a Friday, the day before the Sabbath: the Jewish day of rest. All preparations therefore had to be carried out before sundown. Jesus dies at the ninth hour which is 3pm. 'About three in the afternoon Jesus cried out in a loud voice, "Eli, Eli, lema sabachthani?" which means, "My God, my God, why have you forsaken me?". And when Jesus had cried out again in a loud voice, he gave up his spirit' (Psalm 22.1 in Matthew 27.46, Matthew 27.50). Sometime before sundown Jesus' side was pierced with a lance 'bringing a sudden flow of blood and water' (John 19.34). Permission was given to Joseph of Arimathea for Jesus' body to be taken down from the cross and buried (John 19.38).

In this Station, Jesus' mother Mary is seen holding her dead son, whose lifeless body is stretched stiff from the task of being pinned to the cross. Jesus is unrecognisable (Isaiah 52.14) from the beautiful man he once was (John 1.14), as his face is so disfigured with dried encrusted blood. Mary reaches round to hold her son's body, placing her hand beneath his pierced side from which flows the blood and water of death, a sign of the complete giving of his life for the whole world. Mary's face is also swollen with grief and awash with tears. This is the boy she was given to know and love from his time in her womb. Now all his life is spent and utterly crushed.

Exactly twenty centuries later a tyrant came to power in a country broken by defeat in the First World War. The Germans had initiated the war but were now crushed by the Treaty of Versailles' unrealistic demands for reparations. The Fuhrer's tyranny was a governance built on hatred and violence against all voices of dissension but aimed especially against the Jewish people who flourished and were highly successful.

Separated from other Germans, Jews were herded to the outskirts of their towns and villages. Made to undress, they were then taken to the edge of large dugout pits and shot. The volleys of lead were not always accurate: many were wounded and lived on for hours. The first round of people shot would be asphyxiated by the weight of succeeding bodies. Occasionally if the bullet wasn't fatal, the last line of people to be shot had a chance to escape if they feigned death. Though wounded and naked, a young person might claw their way out of the pit at night and flee into the woods, begging assistance from local farmers. Some made their way back to the ghetto to warn their families, where they were not believed as many clung onto the desperate hope that if they worked, they might have a chance of survival. Others fled, seeing no purpose in returning and lived the life of a fugitive, trying to make passage to Haifa in Israel.

In this Station the pit is almost full. The last line of victims stand on the edge of the pit awaiting their fate. A young couple sit together holding hands in absolute sadness. The woman is half way through her pregnancy, the fruit of her love for her husband. The young man stares down at the writhing mass of people crying out for help. He knows that he soon will be one of them. The love and promise of this couple has been taken away from them.

Jean Lamb

57

Meditation

Jesus has died. His bruised and bleeding body, contorted through suffering, leaves us no doubt. His mother, numb with grief, cradles him again as once she did in Bethlehem. His self oblation is complete: "It is Finished" (John 19.30), he cried out in his dying breath. Has he finished in failure? It could easily seem so.

His mother, his followers and close friends would surely have felt the same. It was finished in more ways than one. Did Jesus himself query his purpose? Could his death succeed in bringing new life? In the grave: in the depths of the underworld did he question? Did he sense himself to be truly abandoned by his Father? "What is my purpose in this hideous place? Has my life on earth been just like any other, over and gone now: pointless? Did I get it wrong and so fall unknowingly into sin?" Were these the unimaginable temptations, undergone on our behalf, when Jesus descended to hell? We cannot know. Perhaps the psalmist had foresight:

> Jesus: 'To you, Lord, I called; to the Lord I cried for mercy: "What is gained if I am silenced, if I go down to the pit? Will the dust praise you? Will it proclaim your faithfulness?"' (Ps 30.8-9) "But now, Lord, what do I look for? My hope is in you. Surely everyone is but a breath. I dwell with you as a foreigner, a stranger, as all my ancestors were" (Ps 39.7,11,12)

Most certainly then, when Jesus died, he would have experienced the horror of apparent meaninglessness and the threat of extinction, which every human eventually must face. In his divine omniscience it might also have been shown to him all that still lay ahead in the way of suffering and the ongoing work of atonement his followers would be called on to share in, before evil could be finally overcome.

All of that, however, is supremely his work, for without him, no one could win through or even take a single step.

The dead Christ before us here faces towards the full horror of what was to come in Holocaust times. The naked couple, suggestive of Adam and Eve again, look at the newly dead. That is their destiny too. Sin, their primal sin, brought death into the world. Even Jesus, the Second Adam, did not exempt himself from death. Yet 'as in Adam all die, so in Christ all will be made alive' (1 Corinthians 15.22). Death cannot be the final end. Once more the psalmist shows us that the sufferings of God's chosen people will one day be validated and redressed:

> Jews: 'Do all the evildoers know nothing? They devour my people as though eating bread; they never call on the Lord. But there they are, overwhelmed with dread, for God is present in the company of the righteous' (Ps 14.4-5) 'Save your people and bless your inheritance; be their shepherd and carry them forever' (Ps 28.9)

Such a prayer will eventually be honoured with utter certainty at the appointed time. There will then be one flock and one Shepherd for all the redeemed, since the Lord is One and his Name One.

Sister Mary Michael CHC

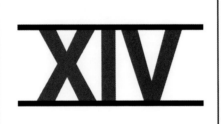

Station of the Holocaust XIV

Jesus is buried in the tomb:
the archangel Michael calls the dead
to rise from their graves

Visual Reflection

Jesus is laid in the tomb of Joseph of Arimathea who was a secret follower of Jesus. He had asked Pontius Pilate for the body of Jesus and laid him in the sepulchre he had built for himself (Matthew 27.58-60). The tomb is well constructed, made out of rock with a large boulder cut as a door (Luke 23.53). The required rituals of perfuming and embalming the body would have to wait until the third day, the day after the Sabbath, as night was falling (John 19.39-40). Jesus is laid out on the slab in the tomb and left alone.

We do not know how many hours Jesus lay there dead, separated from his Heavenly Father. Tradition holds that sometime on the Sabbath, Jesus' soul was kindled by the Holy Spirit. As his life begins again, Jesus' first act of redemption is to voluntarily step down into Sheol, the place of the dead. There Jesus rescues Adam and Eve from their first sentence of banishment from the Garden of Eden. He preaches to all the dead, telling them the joyful news that their sentence of death is not forever (1 Peter 4.6). God's Holy Spirit is working through Jesus' body to bring about their total resurrection, not just of their souls but the very fabric of their bodies (Matthew 27.51-52).

So Jesus' soul meditates on the resurrection of all flesh which had already begun during the earthquake at his death and which will continue through the call of the archangel Michael: '"At that time Michael, the great prince who protects your people, will arise. There will be a time of distress such as has not happened from the beginning of nations until then. But at that time your people - everyone whose name is found written in the book - will be delivered. Multitudes who sleep in the dust of the earth will awake: some to everlasting contempt. Those who are wise will shine like the brightness of the heavens, and those who lead many to righteousness, like the stars for ever and ever."'(Daniel 12.1-3)

The Jewish people are not to be swallowed up by death: God is still enacting his plan out through them. Forty-two people rise from the graves, to transform the forty wilderness years in the desert into a song of rejoicing. As they move out of their graves, the grass of the earth moves to form rays of light emanating from the Glory of Heaven. On the horizon are the twelve Trees of Life (Revelation 22.2), whose fruits are renewed every month and whose leaves are given for the healing of the nations. All peoples who love God will arise and eat of the fruit of healing and health and be touched by the leaves which will renew their once broken lives on earth.

So sacred is every person's life that God will not abandon anybody who wishes to turn to him, even at this last moment at the end of time. Around the action of the resurrection sing the seven seraphim and cherubim, chanting 'Holy Holy Holy is the Lord God Almighty, the whole earth is full of his glory' (Isaiah 6.3). This is the Jubilee of the Lord.

Jean Lamb

Meditation

In the fullness of his humanity Jesus is dead. Since he had power to lay down his life he also had power to take it up again, a charge received from his Father and enabled by the Holy Spirit, Ruach HaQodesh. This waiting space of the Great Sabbath, when the body of Yeshua Ha Mashiach, Jesus, the Messiah, lay in the tomb, was certainly long for those who mourned him in dark perplexity. We in turn lower our eyes to perceive him there, prostrate in the grave.

There are stretches of time in every human life when the enigma of acute, inexplicable suffering weighs heavily and the perceived finality of death fills us with paralysing dread. Each year the Christian Liturgy replays the drama of Christ's suffering, death and rising. Holy Saturday, before the dawn of Easter Day, is long and somehow empty, like the time after a funeral when the mourners feel lost and aimless, unable to re-find the ordinariness of daily living. All the same, glimmers of light and of resurrection promise seep through the liturgical texts. Once more, in this context, the psalmist seems to speak in the person of Jesus as he too awaits resurrection:

Jesus: 'Though you have made me see troubles, many and bitter, you will restore my life again; from the depths of the earth you will again bring me up' (Ps 71.20) 'My body also will rest secure, because you will not abandon me to the realm of the dead, nor will you let your faithful one see decay' (Ps 16.9-10) 'I lie down and sleep; I wake again, because the Lord sustains me' (Ps 3.5) 'Lord my God, I called to you for help, and you healed me. You, Lord, brought me up from the realm of the dead; you spared me from going down to the pit' (Ps 30.2-3)

Such a confident hope is depicted for us here in the last Station. A vision of true everlasting life, forming itself in the consciousness of the dead Christ, is already becoming a universal reality. The dead are beginning to stir. Michael, Guardian of the Jewish people and of the dying, rouses the Holocaust dead. He stands in regal purple with arms outstretched. "Who is like God?" he cries, for this is the very meaning of his name. "Not me", replies his witness; "but the rising Jesus, soon to manifest himself in his full glory." The Holocaust dead can partake of this burgeoning hope as the psalmist shows us on their behalf:

Jews: 'Do you show your wonders to the dead? Do their spirits rise up and praise you? Is your love declared in the grave, your faithfulness in Destruction? Are your wonders known in the place of darkness, or your righteous deeds in the land of oblivion?' (Ps 88.10-12) 'Awake, Lord! Why do you sleep? Rouse yourself! Do not reject us forever. Why do you hide your face and forget our misery and oppression? We are brought down to the dust; our bodies cling to the ground. Rise up and help us; rescue us because of your unfailing love' (Ps 44.23-26) 'Praise be to the Lord, who has not let us be torn by their teeth. We have escaped like a bird from the fowler's snare; the snare has been broken, and we have escaped' (Ps 124.6-7)

We see that the Guardian angels of the once dead children are at hand ready to carry them to heaven where they will behold the face of their Father (Matthew 18.10). Let none of us, then, be afraid. Death does not have the last word, ALLELUIA!

Sister Mary Michael CHC

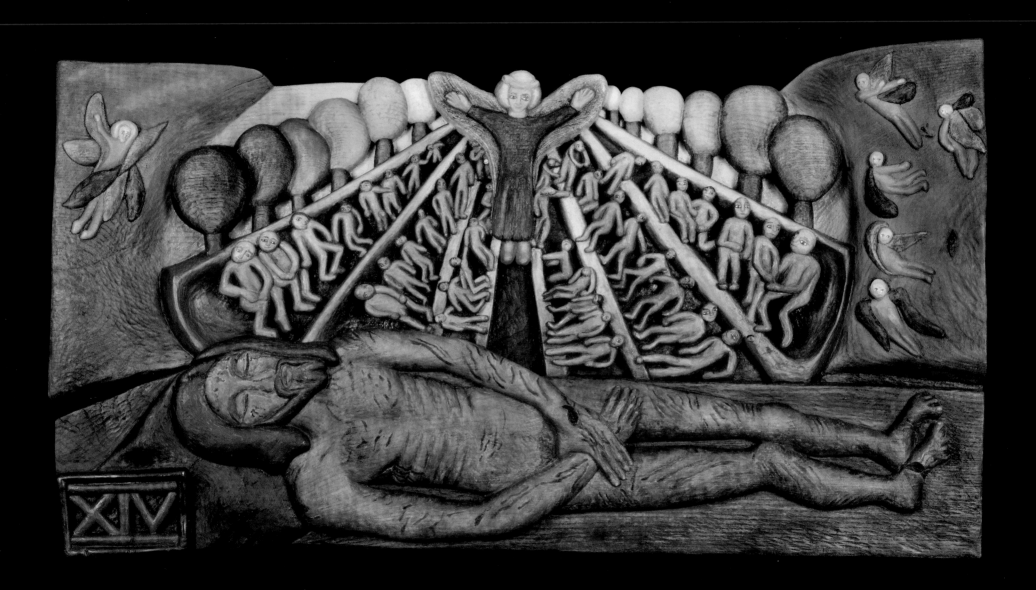

Given the long association of the history of Christian anti-Judaism with the development of Nazi ideology, the decision of the artist and priest Jean Lamb to situate her carvings of the Stations of the Cross in the context of the Holocaust is bold and courageous. There may be those, both Jew and Christian, who will take offense. Jews who understand the Holocaust as a uniquely Jewish experience may be angered by seeing it 'appropriated' for Christian worship. Christians who treasure the uniqueness of Christ's crucifixion as an historical event may be troubled at finding it placed in the alien surroundings of the twentieth century and of a persecution in which Christians were not the primary victims.

Jean's Stations are less a choice and more of a vocation to which she has been called. They are an expression of the movement of the Spirit since the Holocaust and the foundation of the modern state of Israel, that has led Christians radically to re-examine their assumptions about Jews and Judaism. Before the Holocaust it was all too common for Christians as a dominant culture to see Jews as a peculiar and accursed people, condemned to wander the world or to be confined to the ghetto. Theologians commonly argued that God's Covenant with the Jews had been superseded by the new Covenant in Christ and that the stubborn continuation of the Jews in their faith was an offense to Christians. At worst, Jews were collectively held responsible for 'deciding' the death of Jesus.

Scholars now assess Jesus within his own Jewish context. Arguments between Jesus and 'the Jews' are now understood as debates within the Jewish community and not between Jew and 'Christian'. If it is now obvious to recognise that Jesus and his disciples were all Jews and that Jesus was faithful to the Covenant (if critical of the way some of his contemporaries interpreted it),

that is the mark of how fundamentally most Christian assumptions about Judaism have changed. As the Holocaust theologians Roy and Alice Eckhardt have pointed out, 'Had the Jew Jesus of Nazareth lived in the "right" time and "right" place, he would have been dispatched to a gas chamber' (Long Night's Journey into Day, 2nd ed. 1988). Jean has carved that truth into her Stations.

The original division between Christians and Jews arose within the Jewish community as a disagreement over whether Jesus was the Messiah. As a disagreement within the family it was all the more bitter. The admission into the Church of Gentiles who did not need first to be circumcised divided the Church yet further from Israel, the original 'People of God'. The Letter to the Hebrews treated the first Covenant as now 'obsolete' and 'abolished' (Heb. 8.13, 10.9). The dominant Christian outlook on Judaism became 'supersessionist': that 'what is obsolete and outdated will soon disappear' (Heb. 8.13). The destruction of the Temple and the burning of Jerusalem in AD 70 were easily understood as confirmation of the ending of God's relationship with his people, or even as punishment for their rejection of Jesus as the Christ.

The Jews themselves recovered their identity out of the wreckage of dispersion and exile and forged a new way forward as people focussed on book and prayer rather than Temple sacrifice. The parting of the ways and the mutual hardening of hearts was only exacerbated by the establishment of Christianity as the state religion by Constantine in the fourth century, opening the way to persecution of the Jews. Here, with intermittent intensification and relaxation of conflict, theological relations between Christians and Jews remained until the mid twentieth century. Although some Christian communities colluded in its implementation, the

Holocaust itself was less a Christian phenomenon than an intense form of viciously ideological nationalism.

Crucially, the Second Vatican Council reversed older theological and cultural assumptions in its 'Declaration on the Relationship of the Church to Non-Christian Religions', Nostra Aetate (1965), in which the Church proclaims her unity with the chosen people of the Old Testament: 'The Church cannot forget that she received the revelation of the Old Testament through the people with whom God in his inexpressible mercy designed to establish the Ancient Covenant' (N.A. 4). Supersessionist assumptions are replaced with a reliance on the teaching of St Paul. In the Letter to the Romans, Paul employs the image of the cultivated olive tree (Rom. 11.17-24) which has lost branches (the unbelieving Jews) but wild branches grafted in their place (the believing Gentiles). Speaking of the first Covenant as the root of the tree, he reminds the Roman Christians not to boast: 'Do not consider yourself to be superior to those other branches. If you do, consider this: you do not support the root, but the root supports you' (Rom. 11.18). Even if the Gospel is the fulfilment of the Law, it cannot dispose of its antecedent because it is built upon it. The old Covenant is made new without being abolished.

Paul summarises the gifts that the Jews retain: 'The people of Israel. Theirs is the adoption to sonship; theirs the divine glory, the Covenants, the receiving of the Law, the Temple worship and the promises. Theirs are the patriarchs, and from them is traced the human ancestry of the Messiah, who is God over all' (Rom. 9.4-5). He is utterly confident that in the fullness of time God will gather in all his people, including the Jews: 'For God's gifts and his call are irrevocable' (Rom. 11.29). Just as God's people the Jews had been repeatedly disobedient and unfaithful to the Covenant, so too were God's people the Gentiles, but God extends his mercy to them all: 'Just as you who were at one time disobedient to God have now received mercy as a result of their disobedience, so they too have now become disobedient in order that they too may now receive mercy as a result of God's mercy to you. For God has bound everyone over to disobedience so that he may have mercy on them all. "Oh, the depth of the riches of the wisdom and knowledge of God! How unsearchable his judgements and his paths beyond tracing out!"' (Rom. 11.30-33).

Whether they are Jews or Greeks, it is axiomatic for Paul that although they will be unfaithful to God's Covenant, nevertheless God will be faithful to them (Rom. 3.3). Just as God in the Old Testament repeatedly called his people out from their disobedience, so must he do with the new Israel, that is the Church. This Gospel community has never fulfilled the demands of the Gospel even as the community of the first Covenant never fulfilled its demands, but God has mercy on them all.

St Paul's insistence on the irrevocable faithfulness of God to his people was demonstrated over and again in the Hebrew Scriptures. Jean's Stations of the Holocaust however, following the witness of the New Testament, insist on something further: that the divine faithfulness to the Jews is manifest in Jesus Christ. Jesus fully identifies himself with his own people in his insistence that he was sent first to call the house of Israel back to God (Mt. 10.6, 23; 15.24). His understanding of his own messianic vocation and suffering was a necessary part of the fulfilment foretold in the Hebrew Scriptures. As soon as Peter confessed him as the Messiah, Jesus warned his disciples: 'The Son of Man must suffer many things and be rejected by the elders, the chief priests and the teachers of the law, and he must be killed and on the third day be raised to life' (Lk. 9.22).

On the road to Emmaus, Jesus both embodies and preaches the prophecies: '"How foolish you are, and how slow to believe all that the prophets have spoken! Did not the Messiah have to suffer these things and then enter his glory?" And beginning with Moses and all the Prophets, he explained to them what was said in all the Scriptures concerning himself' (Lk. 24.25-27). Both St Matthew and St Luke link Christ's suffering particularly with that of the 'suffering servant' of Isaiah 53 (Mt. 8.17, Acts 8.32-35, also Jn. 1.29). The self offering for his people of the Messiah who is both Son of God and Son of Man cannot be confined by time or geography. The One who died on the cross of Golgotha for the sins of his own people and of all people is present also with them in Auschwitz and wherever his people are suffering and dying.

This radical sense of Jesus' faithfulness to his people can be found even in one of the texts most often cited to explain the Church's historic persecution of the Jews. When Pilate washed his hands of guilt for the death of Jesus, the crowd of Jewish people responded, '"His blood is on us and on our children!"' (Mt. 27.25). Rather than seeing this as an assumption of guilt for his death, we can see this in the context of the Day of Atonement and the sprinkling of the blood of the sacrificial animal on the people to cover their sins and to cleanse the people (Lev. 16, Heb. 9, 10). As John the Baptist proclaims, 'Look, the Lamb of God, who takes away the sin of the world!' (Jn. 1.29). Early on in her Stations (II), Jean makes a point connecting the pouring of the blood of the Messiah on the sufferers in the camps. His and their sufferings are one.

The relationship between prophecy in the first Covenant and fulfilment in the new Covenant raises a critical issue. Many contemporary Biblical scholars have argued that if we are to understand the Scriptures in their own context and according to the best scholarly methods, we can claim no such link. The Hebrew prophets could not foresee Jesus Christ. The fulfilment texts in the New Testament were thus a Christian interpretation of and imposition on the texts that modern readers should not accept. This is a particularly problematic position for Christian readers as it dismisses the entire typological framework of prophecy and fulfilment which has shaped the Church's theology and lectionaries from the earliest times. It drives a Marcionite division between the Old and New Testaments, breaking asunder the wild branches of the Gentiles from St Paul's olive tree.

This quasi-scientific approach also undermines the theology of these Stations of the Holocaust and Sr Mary Michael's interpretation of them. Her reading of the passion narrative is infinitely enriched by her extensive use of the Psalms, the first hymn book of the Temple and of the Church. Traditionally held to have been composed by King David and to refer prophetically to the Son of David, the Psalms read in the light of Christ are inexhaustibly rich and powerfully link the life, death, and resurrection of God's son with the experience of God's people. Happily there is a new generation of Biblical scholars (like Ellen F. Davis in Wondrous Depth: Preaching the Old Testament) who encourage the recovery of pre-modern exegesis without discarding the insights of critical readings.

It must be acknowledged that at times Biblical typology has been used to insist on the supersession of the first Covenant, to see fulfilment as replacement rather than as a treasury containing what is new and what is old (Mt. 13.52). Equally typology has been used to affirm the place of the Jews in the economy of

God's salvation. The medieval Benedictine mystagogue Rupert of Deutz (1075-1129) was known for his anti-Jewish polemic, but he also had this to say in response to Jeremiah 29.11 ('I have plans to prosper you and not to harm you'):

> Verily, his thoughts are those of peace, for he promises to admit to the banquet of his grace the Jews, who are his brethren according to the flesh; thus realising what had been prefigured in the history of the patriarch Joseph. The brethren of Joseph, having sold him, came to him, when they were tormented by hunger; for then he ruled over the whole land of Egypt; he recognised them, he received them, and made, together with them, a great feast; so too, our Lord who is reigning over the whole earth, and is giving the bread of life, in abundance, to the Egyptians (that is, to the Gentiles), will see coming to him the remnants of the children of Israel. He, whom they had denied and put to death, will admit them to his favour, will give them a place at his table, and the true Joseph will feast delightedly with his brethren.

So interpreted, the whole of the Scriptures can be used as a force for unity and reconciliation between God's separated children.

Another force for recognising the common ground shared by Christians and Jews is the current revival in Temple studies, primarily through the many works of Margaret Barker. The Jerusalem Temple was the focus of all Hebrew worship and of the sacrificial cult. More important still, it (like its predecessor the Tent of Meeting) was the visible sign of God's abiding presence, the meeting place of the Lord with his people: 'I have chosen and consecrated this Temple so that my Name may be there for ever. My eyes and my heart will always be there' (2 Chron. 7.16). Even today, all synagogues in the world are oriented towards the Temple Mount so that prayer is made towards that place.

Christians in our own day have tended to dismiss the significance of the Temple as superseded by Jesus and the Church. Jesus foretold the destruction of the Temple (Mk. 13.1-4) and spoke of his own body as the Temple (Jn. 2.19-21). St Paul told the Corinthians to think of their own bodies as a temple (1 Cor. 6.19). Jesus himself was the true Temple as the presence of God in flesh among God's people. Nevertheless the Church did continue to express the reality of this presence in terms of the Temple. It remains the operative metaphor for the encounter with God in the Gospels, in Paul, in Hebrews, and in Revelation. Christian church buildings have throughout their history incorporated architectural elements linking the Church's worship to the Temple.

Whereas after the destruction of the Temple, Rabbinic Judaism focused on study of the Torah, prayer and good works, John McDade points out that 'Christ-centred Jews, guided by Jesus' spiritual and moral radicalisation of Torah observance (loving not only neighbours but enemies) and his disregard of aspects of Torah observance touching on purity and separation, draw instead upon the cultic and sacrificial cult of the Temple worship for their interpretation of the death of Jesus. The community came to understand that the events on the Mount of Calvary should be interpreted in the light of the priestly atoning ritual on the Mount of the Temple.' St Paul describes Jesus himself as the Mercy Seat (the place of God's throne in the Holy of Holies) and his blood as shed for the atonement of sins (Rom. 3.25).

These Stations remind us that where the presence of the Lord is, there is his Temple. The Temple is also the place of divine disclosure, where eternal realities are revealed in an earthly setting, as in Station VI. Here Veronica's veil discloses that the suffering of God is known in the suffering of his little ones, for 'Whoever welcomes one such child in my name welcomes me' (Mt. 18.5). The railway line, like Jesus' cross, becomes a ladder from earth to heaven, and the angels ascending and descending the ladder are the children who have been through the great fires of Birkenau. They become radiant worshippers in the heavenly Temple:

> These are they who have come out of the great tribulation; they have washed their robes and made them white in the blood of the Lamb. Therefore, they are before the throne of God, and serve him day and night in his temple; and he who sits on the throne will shelter them with his presence. Never again will they hunger; never again will they thirst. The sun will not beat down on them, nor any scorching heat. For the Lamb at the centre of the throne will be their shepherd; he will lead them to springs of living water. And God will wipe away every tear from their eyes (Rev. 7.14-17)

This image holds the promise that God transforms the suffering of the innocent into glory through the infinite mercy and justice of our suffering Saviour.

The stripping of Jesus in Station X provides a different kind of disclosure and revelation. Here the ironies pile on top of one another, for the beaten, humiliated, condemned Jesus is revealed as the Second Adam: Man restored to his full dignity and beauty because he, unlike the first Adam, has trod the path of obedience.

All around him are the violent consequences of that first disobedience he was sent to redeem. His seamless robe is the Jewish prayer shawl, the talit, or 'little tent' that for each of the faithful is the Tent of Meeting that was the predecessor of the Temple. The talit also alludes to the Veil of the Temple that will part at Jesus' death, showing that the way is now open from earth to heaven. He is the meeting place of God and Man, of heaven and earth.

The transforming power of his saving death is made manifest in Station XIV, where the resurrection hope proclaimed in the Revelation to John in the setting of the Temple that is the heavenly Jerusalem. Through the self-giving sacrifice of the Christ, the Holocaust dead and the dead of all peoples rise to new and unending life: 'Very truly I tell you, unless a grain of wheat falls to the ground and dies, it remains only a single seed. But if it dies, it produces many seeds' (Jn. 12.24). That fruitfulness is the harvest of souls at the resurrection:

> Then the angel showed me the river of the water of life, as clear as crystal, flowing from the throne of God and of the Lamb down the middle of the great street of the city. On each side of the river stood the tree of life, bearing twelve crops of fruit, yielding its fruit every month. And the leaves of the tree are for healing of the nations. No longer will there be any curse. The throne of God and of the Lamb will be in the city, and his servants will serve him. They will see his face, and his name will be on their foreheads (Rev. 22.1-4)

The heavenly temple is the Garden of Eden restored. There is the river of blessings (Gen. 2.10, Ps. 46.4). The tree of the cross has become again the tree of life in its twelve forms (Ezek. 47.12). The privilege of the Great High Priest to stand before the face of God in the Holy of Holies with the name of God on his forehead (Ex. 28.36-38) now belongs to the whole people of God. The worshippers of God reign with him in eternal triumph.

The Stations will find their way into various places and churches. There they will enable worshippers to walk as pilgrims the Way of the Cross with Jesus and with the victims of the Holocaust. Traditionally, the Stations of the Cross trace a path in the church from the northeast part of the nave to the northwest end (the first seven) and from the southwest to the southeast of the nave (the second seven). This pathway proceeds widdershins, anticlockwise, powerfully contradicting the natural pathway through the building that follows the path of the sun, from east across the south to the west. This contradiction points to humankind's revolt against God and against their own given nature in the image and likeness of God in the killing of his Son. But God says 'No' to humankind's 'No' and brings resolution and healing in the face of revolution and hatred.

The impact of the Stations will be powerful wherever they are displayed. Jean reminds those following the Way of the Cross that Jesus' saving passion and death are not confined to one moment of history but are eternally present in the life of the world. He suffered and died with the victims of the concentration camps. He suffers and dies with all innocent victims of violence, fear, and hatred today. He remains the Jew, Jesus of Nazareth, but to Christians he is also the Messiah who fulfils the mission of Israel to be the one who carries the sins of the nations and brings God's healing and redemption to all people.

Other designs of the Stations of the Cross frequently cushion or spiritualise the impact of Christ's suffering and death. Jean Lamb does not protect the viewers, but allows the horrors of the cross and of the Holocaust to have their full and harrowing impact. Yet in their entirety and because of her honesty, these Stations powerfully convey Christ's healing and redemption. Let us pray that they will also play their role in re-establishing common ground between Christian and Jew and help Christians acknowledge that through Jesus of Nazareth our God has graciously extended his original irrevocable call and promise to the Jews to the Gentiles also. Let us rejoice together in the brotherhood and sisterhood of all God's children and share that peace that Jesus came to bring.

Reverend Canon Dr Peter Doll
Norwich Cathedral

Jean Lamb's sculptures derive from her life-long devotion as a Christian and express a sensitivity heightened by compassion, self-discipline and honesty. As she writes:

> Our faith makes one explore the depths of mankind's depravity as set against the beauty of God's world and love. Artists are called to speak the truth and my calling is as a religious artist.

I greatly admire this understanding of the meaning of faith and art. Yet when Jean invited me to write about The Stations of the Holocaust I was hesitant. This is a very difficult work for a Jewish person to contemplate. It arouses raw and painful feelings and I was inclined to turn away. But it is also a brave work which offers links, albeit fraught and disturbing ones, between Christianity and Judaism at a time when sensitivity towards one another and co-operation between the faiths are of the utmost importance. This aim deserves acknowledgement.

The Stations of the Holocaust is a deeply felt testament, an expression of how the artist understands the core meaning of Christianity. It clearly matters to her that her faith should have a universal resonance. The particular connection with the Holocaust is motivated by the experience of visiting and reading about Auschwitz-Birkenau and other death camps. In linking the sufferings of Jesus with the destruction of European Jewry she wants to recognise and respect the sufferings of the Jewish People in the deepest context possible for a Christian. Through a classic form of religious art her sculpture endeavours to create profound connections between our faiths, rooted in the most basic realities of anguish and desecration, compassion and hope, at a moment in history when we need more than ever to listen to one another's stories and understand and cherish each other's humanity. This is a courageous intention.

Jean's sculpture and writing show her knowledge of the progressive horrors of the Holocaust as they developed to include the confinement of Jews in ghettos, the mass shootings, prior to which the victims were often forced to dig their own burial pits, the use of specially designed vans for gassing, the selections, the murder of further millions in gas chambers, the burning of the bodies, and, throughout, the particular and terrible sufferings of children. The sinister role of the railways is made into an important structural motif in several of the works. Jean thus creates connections between each station of the cross and specific stages in the persecution and murder of the Jews of Europe. This is an important contribution to the awareness of the Holocaust and its implications at a time when there is great concern in and beyond the Jewish community about how the Nazi genocide will be remembered after the last survivors have died.

Both in the sculpture itself and in her descriptions of it the artist gives expression to the powerful human longing for love and empathy. She writes in the IVth Station that 'Every mother would move heaven and earth to touch their living child', acknowledging that the separation from loved ones was one of the deepest forms of anguish for the victims of the Nazi Holocaust, as indeed it remains for all who are deprived of their freedom today. She understands Jesus as wanting 'to apply his example of vulnerable love to every situation of oppression in the world' (Station X). Such compassion is at the core of all our faiths and goes to the heart of what it means to be human.

Yet there is a basic difficulty within the very endeavour on which The Stations of the Holocaust is founded. When we want to include others, especially other faiths or peoples, within our own story we need to examine our own feelings very carefully: what are we saying about our own faith and intentions? But we also have a responsibility to consider how being included in such a manner may feel to those 'others' whom we make part of the narrative we tell.

What does it feel like as a Jewish person to see one's story told in the context of the Stations of the Cross? This is an especially sensitive question with regard to the Holocaust. Few Jewish people think of the Holocaust simply as history. For very many of us it is the experience of our closest family. Both my parents fled Nazi Germany in their teens, leaving behind the homes and lives they knew to begin again as refugees in unknown countries. They were among the minority who were fortunate enough to be able to leave with their immediate relatives. Many others lost everything and everybody and found themselves the sole survivors of what had once been thriving congregations. Many communities had no survivors at all. It would be almost impossible to overestimate the impact of the Holocaust on Jewish life and sensitivities.

I am therefore bound to acknowledge that The Stations of the Holocaust is an extremely hard work to ponder, even to look at, from a Jewish perspective. It touches very deep injuries. Though it tries to be sensitive, it also reopens many wounds. There are several reasons for this, all of them deriving from the difficult history of the relationship between Christianity and Judaism.

The very words 'the Jews' ring with an alarming sound when used in the context of the crucifixion. In the late Second Temple period the cross was a form of torture inflicted widely and ruthlessly on the Jewish population of Palestine by the Romans. Indeed, Jesus was crucified as a Jew. When the cross became the symbol of Christianity, it was experienced by Jews as turned against them, the very people who had been its principal victims. From pogroms at Easter, to the Crusades and the Inquisition, to false allegations of ritual murder, to forced conversion on pain of death, Jews were repeatedly attacked and often murdered as 'Christ-killers' and for their failure to embrace Christianity. Countless thousands paid with their lives. Though this is by no means the whole history of Christian Jewish relations, it nevertheless haunts our shared past. Only with Vatican II, which opened in 1962, did the Church formally acknowledge that Judaism was a valid religion in its own right. The visit by Pope John Paul II to Jerusalem in 2000, when he spoke at the Western Wall of his deep sorrow at the suffering caused by anti-Semitism, prayed for forgiveness and committed himself to 'genuine brotherhood with the People of the Covenant' was a further step on the path toward healing.

To see the cross associated with the Holocaust as an expression of shared suffering presents further difficulties. Whereas the Nazi hatred of the Jews, and of gypsies, the disabled and other groups, was primarily racist rather than religious, it found fertile ground across Europe, in particular in Poland and elsewhere in Eastern Europe, because of the centuries-old prevalence of Christian anti-Semitism. The role of the Vatican during the years of the Third Reich was ambivalent at very best and accusations of implicit collaboration remain. In Germany itself very few Christian leaders spoke out against Nazism. Karl Immer, Pastor Niemoller and Dietrich Bonhoeffer and the few others who acted likewise make brave and noble exceptions. The artist's intention may be that the cross should represent shared pain, but it takes a degree of restraint and reflection to get beyond also seeing in its prominence a symbol of the cause of much Jewish misery and death. Also, while the suffering of one can express the sufferings of many, there can never be any equation with the unquantifiable horrors experienced by any group which has been subject to genocide.

Nevertheless, pondering the Stations should remind us how important it is to honour those priests, monks, nuns and ordinary Christians who with quiet courage risked their lives and families to save their fellow human beings and in so doing testify forever to the highest ideals of faith.

A further difficulty lies in the supersessionist tradition in Christian theology, in which the Hebrew Bible and Jewish history are understood as prefiguring Christianity and only finding their true meaning within it. Typographical Christian art has often portrayed scenes from the 'Old' Testament alongside the 'New' to indicate the fulfilment of the former through the latter. Where such use of core stories and texts is made without the recognition that Judaism has integrity and value in its own right, it becomes a form of appropriation. The Stations of the Holocaust may risk being viewed within this tradition, where the cross is seen as giving meaning to the Jewish experience and the Holocaust is given its 'true' significance by the story of the Passion. Such a perception, clearly not meant by the artist, would be literally unbearable for Jews, to whom it would involve betraying their families and communities who were murdered precisely because of their religion.

Though none of these are her intentions, they may help to explain why Jean Lamb's art is likely to touch the Jewish observer in painful

and challenging ways. More than one friend with whom I have spoken has recalled the post-war presence of the Carmelite cross which overlooked the site of Auschwitz-Birkenau, until deeper understanding of how sorely insensitive this could feel led to its being moved to a different location.

Yet these observations, uncomfortable even to set down, should not be the end point of our consideration of Jean's work. Rather, they may help to focus our thoughts in two important directions.

The Bible instructs us to love not only our neighbour but also the stranger, those different from ourselves. But we often remain unaware of the impact of our beliefs and actions on those who have a different faith or way of life from our own. Jean's work challenges us to consider how our symbols, stories and conduct affect others. What does what I say and do through my faith mean for others who may not share it? Is its message as inclusive, just and compassionate as I would like to think? Does it contain subtexts or even overt meanings for others, of which I may be unaware? No one of any faith or nationality can answer these questions without serious reflection and an anxious heart. Yet we have a responsibility to be sensitive to these very real possibilities which challenge us to examine ourselves, our beliefs and the way we express them honestly and deeply.

This leads to the wider concern of how we ought to engage with the histories and stories of others. We can ignore them altogether, treat them as mere curiosities or show plain hostility; the state of our planet is too perilous to make any of these options realistic if we want to create a viable and peaceful future. As the Reverend Dr. Martin Luther King wrote in his remarkable Letter from Birmingham

City Jail, 'We are caught in an inescapable network of mutuality'. Understanding and co-operation between our faiths is therefore an absolute necessity; we have no other realistic choice than to work together for the safety and wellbeing of us all. To do so we need insight into and empathy for each other's stories and symbols; we need to uphold each other's dignity and defend each other's humanity.

Jean Lamb's work engages in a complex and troubling, but in intention, compassionate, manner with these central concerns which are critical not only for the future of Christians and Jews but for civilisation itself. Only if we find ways of including each other within the compass of our understanding of suffering and compassion, dignity and hope, can our faiths have ultimate significance and value for humanity and life as a whole.

Contemplation of the Stations of the Holocaust, whether through prayer, music, pilgrimage or meditation on works of art, has a central place in Christian spirituality. As an outsider, I can only imagine that it has the power to awaken deep compassion for suffering, revulsion against cruelty, and profound humility. Perhaps pondering The Stations of the Holocaust may help awaken such feelings within us towards all those whom we are liable to think of as other, and all those whose humanity, suffering and dignity we might be in danger of failing to perceive.

Rabbi Jonathan Wittenberg

References

References used by Jean Lamb during the preparations and carvings of the Stations of the Holocaust.

Appleman-Jurman Alicia, *Alicia: My Story* (USA: Bantam, 1988)

Barnard Clifford, *Two Weeks in May 1945 Sandbostel Concentration Camp and the Friends Ambulance Unit* (London: Quaker, 1999)

Berr Hélène, *Journal* (Britain: MacLehose Press, 2009)

Birenbaum Halina, *Hope Is The Last To Die* (Oświęcim: State Museum, 1994)

Bontjes van Beek Mietje, *Verbrennt diese Briefe!* (Germany: Atelier im Bauernhaus, 1998)

Evangelical Sisterhood of Mary (ed.), *Christians Repent for 2000 Years of Antisemitism* (Germany: Evangelical Sisterhood of Mary, 2001)

Deselaers Manfred, *"Mein Gott, mein Gott, warum hast du mich verlassen?"* (Germany: Erdtmann, 1996)

Dobschiner Johanna-Ruth, *Selected to Live* (Britain: Marshall Pickering, 1969)

Doorsy Yasmin, *Representations of Auschwitz* (Poland: Auschwitz-Birkenau State Museum, 1995)

Frankl Viktor E., *Man's Search For Meaning* (Britain: Rider, 2004)

Gilbert Martin, *The Holocaust: The Jewish Tragedy* (London: Fontana Press, 1987)

Gilbert Martin, *The Routledge Atlas of the Holocaust* (Britain: Routledge, Bodmin, 2009)

Gollwitzer Helmut, *Dying We Live: The Final Messages and Records of some Germans who Defied Hitler* (London: Fontana, 1974)

Guttman Esther, *Thank God for England: Escape from Nazi Germany* (Britain: Barny Books, 1997)

Kluge Heidelore, *Cato Bontjes Van Beek "Ich will nur eins sein, und das ist ein Mensch : das kurze Leben einer Widerstandskämpferin 1920-1943* (Stuttgart: Urachhaus, 1994)

Levi Primo, *If This is a Man - The Truce* (Britain: Penguin Books, 1979)

Levi Primo, *The Periodic Table* (London: Penguin Books, 1986)

Littell Franklin H., *The Crucifixion of the Jews* (USA: Harper & Row Publishers Inc., 1975)

Lord Russell of Liverpool, *The Scourge of the Swastika* (Britain: Cassell and Company Ltd. 1954)

Shirer William L., *The Rise and Fall of the Third Reich: A History of Nazi Germany* (USA: Simon & Schuster, 1960)

Volavková Hana (ed.), *I Never Saw Another Butterfly* (London: Random House Inc., 1995)

Wiesel Elie, *Night* (USA: Bantam with Hill & Wang, 1960)

Wiesenthal Simon, *The Sunflower: On the Possibilities and Limits of Forgiveness* (USA: Schocken Books Inc., 1997)

Reforences in Sister Mary Michael CHC's Meditations

Shaw Gilbert, *A Pilgrim's Book of Prayers* (Britain: Mowbray 1947)

Singer Rev. S., *The Authorised Daily Prayer Book of the United Hebrew Congregations of the Congregations of the Commonwealth* (Britain: Kuperard Centenary Edition Revised 1998)

References in Reverend Canon Dr Peter Doll's The Stations of the Cross and the Holocaust

Barker Margaret, *The Gate of Heaven: The History and Symbolism of the Temple in Jerusalem* (Britain: Sheffield Phoenix Press Ltd., 2008)

Davis Ellen F., *Wondrous Depth: Preaching the Old Testament* (Britain: Westminster John Knox Press, 2005)

Eckhardt Alice L. and A. Roy Eckhardt, *Long Night's Journey into Day: A Revised Retrospective on the Holocaust* (USA: Wayne State University Press, 1988)

McDade, *John, A Promise Fulfilled, A Ransom Paid* (Britain: The Tablet, 8th October 2005)

Pope Paul VI, *Declaration on the Relationship of the Church to Non-Christian Religions: Nostra Aetate* (The Holy See, Second Vatican Council, 1965)

All Bible quotes in this catalogue are taken, with thanks, from:

The Holy Bible: New International Version (London: Hodder and Stoughton, 2011)

Biographies

Jean Lamb

Jean Lamb is a professional artist and associate priest in the Church of England with over 30 years experience of making art for and with the Christian community. She graduated from Reading University in 1979, specialising in Fine Art (B.A.Hons.) She then continued her studies in Theology, obtaining an Oxford Certificate in Theology from St Stephen's House in 1984. Her postgraduate MA degree was in Fine Art at Nottingham Trent University, 1988.

Sister Mary Michael CHC

Sister Mary Michael has had a life long vocation to pray for Christian Unity, and to work for inter-faith relations through teaching and writing. After obtaining a Diploma in Education 1959, she joined the Anglican Benedictine Community of the Holy Cross in 1961 and was appointed Novice Mistress in 1972. In 2014, she celebrated the Golden Jubilee of her profession. She is an integral part of the serving community at the Holy Cross Convent.

David J Moore

David Moore is retired Methodist Minister who has devoted his life to ecumenism and art. Always socially active, he is co-founder of various organisations, namely Crisis and Alcohol Concern. He studied woodcarving under Santiago Bell, the Chilean artist, activist and political exile, enabling him to discover vocational fulfilment through carving wood, making sculptures and curating exhibitions.

Peter Doll

Peter Doll is a native of Washington D.C. and studied History at Yale University, graduating in 1984. He went on to study Modern History at Oxford University, obtaining a D.Phil in 1989 and specialising in Theology for his MA, 1994. Ordained in 1995, he has served as a parish priest and university chaplain, and is currently Canon Librarian of Norwich Cathedral. He is the author of works on church and state, and ecumenical, architectural, and liturgical history.

John Witcombe

John Witcombe is a pastoral leader in the Anglican Community. After reading Law at Cambridge University, he trained in Theology at Nottingham. His MPhil paper was entitled 'The Correlation of Love and Death in the Theology of Atonement', 1991. John was ordained in 1984, and after a varied ministry in parishes, theological teaching and diocesan vocations and training, became Dean of Coventry in January 2013.

Jonathan Wittenberg

Jonathan Wittenberg was born into a family with a German-Jewish rabbinic background. He read English at Cambridge followed by a PGCE. After two years of teaching he studied for the rabbinate at Leo Baeck College, London and in Jerusalem. Since 1987 he has been rabbi of the New North London Synagogue and Senior Rabbi of Masorti Judaism UK. His books include 'The Eternal Journey: Meditations on the Jewish Year' and 'The Silence of Dark Water; An Inner Journey'. He has been widely involved in interfaith dialogue.

Acknowledgements

David and Annemarie Lamb: supporters of the project
Chrissy and Robert Lake: encouragement and hospitality
Ingelore Behrens: hospitality and historic family information
Reverend Canon Dr Michael Taylor: support during the writing of the catalogue and preparations for the inaugural exhibition

Community of the Holy Cross, Costock: hosting the Stations between 2000 and 2013 with special thanks to Reverend Mother Mary Luke
Sister Mary Michael: intellectual and spiritual support during the making of the Stations and for the writing of the Meditations
Louise Watson: editing and proofreading

Reverend David Moore: exhibiting the stations 2004 to 2012 and for writing in the catalogue
Reverend Canon Dr Peter Doll: artistic appreciation and for writing in the catalogue
Rabbi Jonathan Wittenberg: his writing in the catalogue and for stimulating inter-faith dialogue

David Lamb: further proofreading
Eva McGrath: proofreader, final editor and supporter

With special thanks to Dean John Witcombe for permission to host the inaugural exhibition in Coventry Cathedral and for writing in the catalogue
Thanks to the Coventry Cathedral Community for support and advice before the exhibition and throughout its stay

Kevin Spragget: designing and constructing the exhibition stands
John Straw: building the transportation crates
Henry McGrath: exhibition installation

James Turner: photographer
www.jamesturnerphotography.co.uk

William McGrath: print design and layout for the whole project and for personal assistance
www.willmcgrath.co.uk

Artwork information

The Stations of the Holocaust by Jean Lamb

Carved between 1999 and 2012, the fourteen elm wood reliefs are each approximately 16 inches by 32 inches (40cm x 81cm).

The photographs displayed in this catalogue are of the original elm wood carvings which are painted with oil paint and linseed oil.

The Stations in this exhibition are casts of the originals, made in silicone moulds and with jesmonite plaster. They were painted with oil paint between 2014 and 2015.

The casts are available for sale, either individually or as a set.

Details of other works: including watercolours, wood sculptures, oils and prints can be found on Jean's website.

www.jeanlamb.com